The
Second Baby
Survival Guide

To my husband, Mark, and my children
Harry, Rory, William and Johnny.

The
Second Baby
Survival Guide

NAIA EDWARDS

RODALE

First published 2010 by Rodale
an imprint of Pan Macmillan, a division of Macmillan Publishers Limited
Pan Macmillan, 20 New Wharf Road, London N1 9RR
Basingstoke and Oxford
Associated companies throughout the world
www.panmacmillan.com

ISBN 978-1-9057-4467-1

A CIP catalogue record for this book is available from the British Library.

Text designed by seagulls.net

Printed and bound by CPI Group (UK) Ltd, Croydon, CR0 4YY

This book is intended as a reference volume only, not as a medical manual.
The information given here is designed to help you make informed decisions
about your health. It is not intended as a substitute for any treatment that you
may have been prescribed by your doctor. If you suspect you have a
medical problem, we urge you to seek competent medical help.

Mention of specific companies, organizations or authorities in this book does not
imply endorsement by the publisher, nor does mention of specific companies,
organizations or authorities in the book imply that they endorse the book.

Addresses, websites and telephone numbers given in this book
were correct at the time of going to press.

Visit **www.panmacmillan.com** to read more about all our books and to buy them.
You will also find features, author interviews and news of any author events, and you
can sign up for e-newsletters so that you're always first to hear about our new releases.

We inspire and enable people to improve their lives and the world around them
For more of our products visit **rodalestore.com** or call 800-848-4735

Contents

Acknowledgements

I would like to thank all the parents who gave up their time to tell me – either in writing or in conversation – of their experience of life with two children, and to share their stories, wisdom, advice and tips. This book is a collaboration and could not have been written without them.

Introduction

Like many mothers, I prepared madly both before and after my first child was born. Books were bought and read from cover to cover, advice was sought (and given, even if not asked for), classes were attended, manuals referred to and well-thumbed. But when I became pregnant with my second child I did none of these things. It wasn't exactly that I thought it would be easy having a second child, but I reasoned I'd done it once so I knew what to expect – and I thought my second child would just slot in. Surely we'd been through the most difficult transition of going from having no children to one child, from being independently dependant-less to becoming parents? We knew what it was like to have no sleep, to have only one topic of conversation and to prefer going to bed than going to a party. The transition from one child to two, in comparison, would surely be a walk in the park?

A stumble through the jungle probably more accurately describes it – deeply impenetrable periods with unexpected clear patches of light and calm in between, which when reached gave me a lasting sense of achievement. There were two main things I hadn't bargained on: that my second baby would be so different from my first; and how challenging it would be to look after a new baby while I was also looking after a toddler, not to mention how difficult it can be to look after a toddler while looking after a baby. It is learning how to care for two children, with different needs and requirements, at the same time that is so different and so hard. I hadn't been prepared for the exhaustion, the frustrations, the challenges or the emotions – for the even greater love I could feel for my two children. I needed *more* advice and help, not *less*, when I had my second baby.

Having a second child is not the same as having your first. For a start, you aren't the same person you were first time around. You are definitely older this time (though maybe only a little bit), and wiser – probably quite a lot. Other circumstances may be different too – you may be financially better or worse off, live in a different house, have changed job or stopped working. Your friendships and relationships with your family will have changed too – you probably know more people with babies and young children than you did before (which makes things a lot easier), and you may have become more or less reliant on close family. Your relationship with your partner will have changed too as you became parents. Most importantly of all, you already have that incredibly strong bond with your first child. All these things are different. So it is hardly surprising that having a second child should not be a repeat of the first.

My experience of coping with life with two children, eventually four, will not be the same as yours, as everyone's circumstances are different. How easily you cope with having a second child will depend on such things as the gender of your children, the age gap between them, their health – and yours – and, most importantly, their person-alities. To get as broad a picture as possible, I have spoken to as many parents as I could to find out what it was like for them to have a second child, what tips they could share, what advice they could give and what they wish they'd known before they set out on the journey of becom-ing parents to two children. Every family's story is different; every mother's experience of life with two children unique. Funny, sad, touching, wonderful – I have been truly amazed and inspired by listening to how mothers and families have coped in sometimes very difficult circumstances, which they have related with humour, strength and a calm that I could only ever aspire to. But, while each person has a different story to tell, there are common threads to pick up on too; common concerns in pregnancy about loving their second child as much as their first, common worries about jealousy in their firstborn, similar problems faced when feeding a newborn and trying to entertain a toddler at the same time, typical feelings of guilt about how much less time you have to spend with your second baby compared to your first. I have tried to look at these situations, problems and concerns and offer ways of dealing with them that will be helpful to you as you embark on the second baby journey yourself.

A few days ago, just as I was nearing the end of writing this book, my ten-year-old son, William, came in to see how I was doing. 'Why is your book called a survival guide?' he asked me. He'd just been watching Ray Mears doing impossibly clever things with a few sticks in the middle of nowhere and he didn't quite see what this had to do with bringing up children. Hmmm, good question. Did it sound a bit negative? Well, I thought, there are some times with a new baby and a toddler when just surviving and getting through the day can seem like a huge achievement. So then I looked up 'survival' on the internet where I learned from the experts that the key to survival is preparation. The more prepared you are the easier it is to survive. So that's the answer. The aim of this book is to help you prepare for your second baby with practical advice, tips and the collected wisdom and experience of many parents who have survived, so that you too can not only survive having your second baby, but *enjoy* life with your baby and toddler too.

ONE

Congratulations!
You're pregnant again

I can vividly remember discovering I was pregnant with my second child. We were driving back from staying with my mother-in-law in Norfolk with our twenty-month-old son, Harry, in the back of the car when I had an overwhelming and urgent desire to go to sleep. Admittedly the previous few days of trying to stop our son from accidentally breaking anything of precious value in his grandmother's non-child proof house, and the bracing sea air walks designed to tire Harry out so he'd sleep at something approximating his usual bedtime in an unfamiliar bedroom, had taken their toll on me, but this was not a normal tiredness. It was more like the sort of tiredness I imagined you might feel after climbing Mount Everest – only Norfolk is very flat so I definitely hadn't climbed any mountains; or after drinking too much wine late into the night – but I'd been off wine too, hadn't felt like it. Ah! Bells began to ring – I was pregnant again. And then I fell instantly and deeply asleep.

For me, buying the pregnancy kit and doing the test was a formality so that when the blue line finally confirmed what I already knew, I had had a bit of time to analyse how I felt. It was a mixture of things.

Excited – yes, definitely. We'd wanted a second child – a brother or sister for Harry. Elated and joyous – that too. There is something so miraculous about conceiving a child and knowing that a new life is beginning to form inside you. Relieved – it could happen again, *was* happening. We didn't have to wait for months of trying, only to be disappointed each month like some of my friends. This was it; we were going to have another baby. We were going to be a real family.

But these wonderfully powerful, positive emotions were mixed with other feelings too. The strongest of these was anxiety. What if …? What if I couldn't cope with two, with the night-time feeds and lack of sleep all over again? After all, sometimes I felt as if I wasn't coping well with one. What if Harry hated having a brother or sister and they hated each other? What if I suffered from postnatal depression this time around, even though I hadn't with my first? What if we couldn't really afford it after all? What if it ruined my relationship with my husband? And, the worst fear of all – what if I didn't bond with this baby, and couldn't love it as much as my first child?

All of these fears and mixed emotions are perfectly normal.

Mums on discovering they were pregnant with their second child:

'I had two early miscarriages after my first child was born and I was becoming increasingly desperate for two children. So when I got the news that I was pregnant again, I was anxious and tried not to be too hopeful. But then, when it looked as though this one was going to stay, bizarre as it may sound, I suddenly panicked that maybe we should have stuck with just one. I kept remembering how badly I'd coped with a baby, and how much easier our life was now our *daughter was older. I worried that having a second child would change everything too much and I wondered whether I'd be able to love another baby as much.'*

Kara, mother of Stella and Louis

'When I did the test and discovered I was pregnant with number two my first thought was that we'd have to cancel the summer holiday we'd just booked. Isn't that awful? I've always felt guilty about that. I was very pleased too, though!'

Liz, mother of Joseph and Miles

'I remember when I discovered I was pregnant with my second child, that night I crept into my daughter's bedroom and watched her sleeping. I kept thinking "Am I about to ruin your life?" and feeling terrible. Then I remembered how close I am to my own brother and how glad I am that I have a brother and everything was all right again. I stopped worrying after that.'

Rosie, mother of Anna and James

'Because it took me a long time to get pregnant the first time, we thought it would be the same second time around. I couldn't believe it when I discovered I was pregnant again when my daughter was only six months old. I was really pleased on the one hand, but a bit shocked too and worried that it was all happening again a bit too soon. I worried that I hadn't really had enough time to get used to being a first-time mum, let alone a mother of two.'

Annie, mother of Lily and Sam

'I felt much calmer the second time I discovered I was pregnant. I'd sort of guessed I was pregnant anyway and it felt absolutely right. I wasn't so scared and I was just happy – looking forward to it.'

Gina, mother of Daniel and Finn

'As I'd just had a baby four months beforehand I was in total shock and surprise. Didn't think it was really possible and kept thinking it must have been an immaculate conception!'

Clare, mother of Isabelle, Grace and Sam

Whether you've planned and longed for this second child as I had and want to shout it from the rooftops, or whether this second baby is a surprise that comes earlier or later than you were hoping or just at the wrong time (I'm not sure if there is ever a 'right time') and you need a bit of time before telling even your partner, you are bound to fluctuate from feelings of wild euphoria to near panic. After all, you're pregnant and your hormones are all over the place. (Sorry, that's not meant to sound patronizing, but sometimes it helps to remember that pregnancy hormones do make us much more prone to mood swings.) But whatever you are feeling – congratulations. You are embarking on another hugely important part of your and your family's life.

You've been pregnant before – so no worries?

You've done it all before, know what to expect, have survived it and maybe enjoyed being pregnant before – so doing it all again should be a doddle. Hmmm. Being pregnant for a second time is not the same as being pregnant the first time. But most importantly of all and most obviously the difference is that you are already a mother; you already have a child to look after. And that changes everything – how you feel emotionally and how you manage physically. As Tina, a counsellor and mother of two boys said: 'Looking back on it, I realize just how much time I had when I was pregnant with my first child. I had time to think about everything. I read every book going, and knew what to expect and what was happening to my baby week by week. I was hugely aware of every single change that was happening to my body and gave in to it, doing the right exercises and eating the right things and resting when I felt tired. It was quite an indulgent time really. When I was pregnant with Jason, I had no time at all really to think about how *I* was feeling. I could hardly remember how many weeks pregnant I was, I was far too busy with looking after Oli. There simply wasn't time to think. And no one really asked me how I was feeling either; they just expected that I'd get on with it and asked me how Oliver was feeling. Actually that was great, because the nine months just flew by.'

While for some people, like Tina, the sheer busy-ness of looking after one child means there is no time to worry about being pregnant a second time round, for others, like Rachel, being a mother to her daughter, Sophie, altered the experience of being pregnant again in a different way. 'Until Sophie was born and I held her in my arms, I found it quite difficult to believe that I was actually going to end up with a real baby – my child. I thought of everything in my pregnancy as something that was happening to *me* and how my body was chang- ing. Being pregnant with my second daughter was different. She was a person right from the start – and I thought of everything in terms of what was happening to her and what it would mean for Sophie. My worries were not for me, but how it would affect my two children.'

Being pregnant second time around has advantages and disadvantages. On the plus side, you have been through it once before so some of the weird things that happen to you in pregnancy, which were so worrying the first time, don't worry you at all when they happen again. You are more confident as well as simply having less time to worry.

On the minus side, because you've been through it all before and know what to expect, you may worry more than before (I felt awful last time, can I cope with feeling like that all over again?). On top of that many people will assume you don't need any help because you're an old hand and so you shouldn't have anything to worry about.

Worry checklist on being pregnant second time around

Will I love my second child as much as my first?

You've probably had lots of people give you the same answer. They've told you love expands, has no limits and that of course you will be able to love your second child as much as your first. They say it in a breezy, matter-of-fact sort of way, as if you're mad to doubt it. The trouble is that, while your head tells you that your friends are probably right, your heart finds it difficult to imagine being able to love anyone else as much as you love your first child. But actually you can, although it's not quite as simple as that.

If you think about it, lots of people have two parents – a mother and father whom they have the capacity to love equally. You don't think to yourself, I love my mother so much, there's no room to love my father as much. But what is also true is that you love them differently. And just as you love your mother for the person she is and your father for the person he is, you can love both your children passionately and deeply and equally but differently for the different people they are. I am not promising you will love your children equally – some people find that they do love one child more than another or find one child easier to be with, though not necessarily the first child more than the second. But I do promise that it is absolutely possible and probable that you will love your second child as much as your first without it affecting your love for your first. I have four children who are all very different but the amount of love I have for them all is the same – the love for each of them is not diminished by how many of them there are. If anything, each one seems to increase the amount of love I have for all of them.

However, I should issue a slight word of caution here: you may be one of those people who fall in love with their baby instantly, at first sight and touch and smell. But not everyone does; either first or second time around. The love you have for your first child has had time to deepen and grow over the months as you have got to know each other, and spent time together. Don't expect to love your second child as much as your first straight away – this may happen over the weeks and months as you get to know each other.

Have I got the age gap right?

The most common age gap between first and second children is somewhere between two and three years – thirty-five months to be exact according to the Office for National Statistics. But this, of course, does not mean it is the best interval to have between children – it is simply more likely that just after your child has had their second birthday is when the pressure of questions such as 'When are you thinking of having another?', or 'Will Johnny/Jane be getting a little brother or sister soon?', reaches its peak.

Although attempts have been made to calculate what the optimum period between children might be in terms of reducing sibling rivalry, or for promoting intellectual development, or good health, there is no right or wrong answer. In the end, the right age gap is the one that is right for you. The age gap will make a difference to the relationship between the children and their relationship with you, but whatever that age gap is, it will have its own set of advantages and disadvantages:

● *Age gap of less than two years*
The advantages are that you will get the baby stage, which many people find the most physically exhausting (the night feeds, the nappies), over with more quickly. Having children so close together in age means that they are more likely to be able to share and enjoy the same toys (and more likely to fight over them too, of course), will be at the same developmental level and therefore will enjoy doing the same things, hopefully playing happily together. Another advantage of having two children very close together is that, to begin with anyway, jealousy is minimized. As Sarah, now mother of four boys explained to me: 'Fergus was thirteen months and not walking or making any attempt to, when Miles was born. So I had two babies together; I just had one baby bigger than the other. Bringing Miles home was just coming back from hospital to normality for me! There was no jealousy or settling problems with Ferg as he didn't know what was happening.'

The disadvantages are that this gap is very hard work. Your body has scarcely had time to recover from the first pregnancy and your iron stores may be pretty low still, making you much more tired. Your first child may still be waking up in the night and your baby certainly will, and you have to try and juggle daytime naps too. Quite apart from that, you need hugely strong biceps for carrying two little ones around the house.

● *Age gap of between two and four years*
Again, the advantages are that your children are still close enough in age to enjoy doing a lot of things together and may well entertain each other as they get a bit older, leaving you time to get on and do other things. It is thought that children who have this gap may well become very close and good friends with each other. Also, a child of between two and four years of age is more able to understand what you tell them and to explain to you how they are feeling ('I hate my brother and want to bash him over the head with a saucepan!'), which can make it easier to help them. At this age, children are beginning to become more independent and to be able to do more things for themselves and to help you (getting dressed, going to the loo, etc.).

Of course, the biggest disadvantage of this age gap is also that a child of two years plus is becoming more independent and is longing to do things without your help – which takes twice as long and requires the patience of a whole host of saints. The frustration and angry shouts and tantrums (i.e. the Terrible Twos), which occur if you try and interfere with their dressing skills – no doubt waking the baby you have just so carefully got to sleep – are an everyday factor of this age difference, at least for a while in the early days.

● *Age gap of five years or more*
The huge advantage of this age gap is that you have a lot more time to give your attention to both children. While your child of five years plus is at school during the day you can coo over your baby as much as you like without fear of upsetting your elder child – and sleep, too, while your baby sleeps. Then, when your older child comes home from

school you can give them all your attention without feeling guilty about neglecting the baby who's had your attention all day. Your five year old may like helping to look after the baby and, in later life, may develop a very good relationship with their sibling.

The disadvantage is that being so far apart in age the children will not want to do the same things, nor share the same friends or toys. It can mean that you tend to do fewer things together as a family because of the different needs: Dad takes six year old to play football, Mum takes one year old to baby and toddler group, that sort of thing.

Will my elder child love having a new brother or sister?

One reason most of us have more than one child is because we want to provide our first child with a friend, a playmate, someone to share family life with and to love for life. We want our children to be close and to love each other. But it is impossible to guarantee. Some children will love having a baby brother or sister from the moment they set eyes on them. They'll love stroking them, and pushing them in the pram and giving them a jammy finger to suck or a battered teddy to put in the cot at night and reading to them from an upside down book. Others will either take no notice or actively dislike them and try to poke them to see if the baby will cry when you're not looking. Then as your children get older things may change. The jealous child begins to see the advantage in having a clever younger brother and they will become friends. Equally, the child who was so obsessed with the baby may feel less loving when the baby stops being so placidly obedient. Children who fight fiercely all through their early childhood may become incredibly close in their teens or even once they've left home (as I did with my sister).

And whether your children like each other and become friends will not really be down to how far apart they are in age, but will have much more to do with their personalities and temperament. Even gender doesn't seem to make a great difference. A girl and a boy can be a great mix, especially if the elder child is a girl and displays her mothering instinct by wanting to protect and look after her younger brother. Two girls or two boys may have the same interests and likes in common, which can lead to them being closer, but it can also lead to a more competitive relationship and jealousy. There is simply no knowing. You can help them be nice to each other, and teach them how to have respect for each other, but you cannot make them like each other.

But that doesn't mean you shouldn't have given your elder child a sibling. Yes, children without siblings have some advantages – they have more of your undivided attention more of the time and you have more money to spend on them. But siblings learn how to share (eventually), how to wait their turn, how to play together, how to resolve conflict.

The physical side of pregnancy second time around

Because you've already been pregnant before, the chances are that you'll recognize the symptoms of being pregnant earlier, especially if you're looking for them. Whether it's suddenly noticing that you've become extra sensitive to certain smells, or things taste different, or you can't make that journey to your sister's house only five minutes away without needing to stop for a wee, or you notice your bra does-n't fit quite as well as it did yesterday. From that moment on, all the sensations and feelings of pregnancy, which may have become a distant memory, come forcibly flooding back. This may or may not fill you with joy depending on how you felt when you were pregnant first time around. But if you had a difficult time, the good news is that it doesn't follow that it will be difficult this time around. Your second pregnancy may affect you quite differently and you could sail through it this time – second pregnancies are often easier.

Because your muscles, skin and joints have been stretched and pulled and loosened already, you will notice some other changes too. Everything seems to happen earlier than it did the first time: feeling pregnant, looking pregnant, feeling your baby's butterfly kiss kicks and hearing the heartbeat. All these things are wonderful – well, feeling your baby's presence earlier anyway, if not the feeling and looking pregnant bit.

What's different

● *Needing to wee – all the time*

You know you're pregnant again when you start having to go for a wee every five minutes. And you may need to go even more frequently than before owing to those weaker muscles. Luckily this doesn't last so long – as your uterus moves out of the pelvis sooner than before, the pressure on your bladder is relieved quicker too. Another plus: you can always use your toddler as an excuse for why you're carrying a potty around with you wherever you go.

● *Tender breasts*

Feeling tenderness in your breasts or noticing that they have got larger may be another change that alerts you to the fact that you might be pregnant – just as it did the first time. The difference, second time round, is that you might still be feeding your firstborn. If you are, there's no need to stop feeding. You can continue to do this right through your pregnancy, and even afterwards if you wish to.

● *Showing early*

It's amazing how early on you can start to look pregnant with number two. Be prepared to start searching for those attractive stretchy maternity trousers you'd buried at the back of your cupboards by the time you're twelve weeks – despite the fact that your baby is still only 5 centimetres (2 inches) long! Unless you've been eating a lot more than normal, the bulge really is your baby. The reason why you look bigger so much earlier is not because your baby is necessarily going to be bigger, but because your muscles are less good at keeping your uterus in place, as it moves up out of your pelvis sooner.

● *Morning sickness*

If you spent the first three months or more rushing to the loo to be sick with your first baby, then I'm afraid the chances are that you'll be doing this again with your second, though the good news is that it probably won't be quite so severe. Having said that, the experience of being sick is not made easier with a toddler watching over you anxiously.

If you weren't sick first time around, this doesn't guarantee you won't be now. It will come as a shock if you haven't had morning sickness before, especially to find that it isn't confined to the morning – you can feel sick at any time of day. It may help to remember firstly that in most cases you stop feeling sick after twelve weeks and secondly that however ghastly you're feeling, the baby is fine.

For those of you who don't experience it at all, just be thankful.

● *Swelling and pre-eclampsia*

The chances are that you developed some swelling in your legs, hands and feet the first time you were pregnant as 60 to 70 per cent of all pregnant women do. If it happened first time, then it's likely to happen again, especially as you will probably be on your feet more, but provided you don't put on too much weight it's nothing to worry about. Make sure you do put your feet up – literally – as often as you can, and try not to wear socks or stockings that have tight elastic around the top. This may help to prevent you getting varicose veins in your legs or at least to make you more comfortable if you do suffer from them.

If you get sudden swelling in other parts of your body, you need to see your midwife, especially if you had pre-eclampsia the first time, because there's a 10 per cent chance of it reoccurring. The risk is low if you didn't have it first time, although for some reason it's slightly higher if you have a different partner second time round. You are also more likely to have pre-eclampsia in a second pregnancy if:

* you had a premature first baby
* you have diabetes
* you are black
* you have chronic high blood pressure
* you are overweight.

Do make sure you go to all your antenatal appointments where your blood pressure and urine will be checked for signs of pre-eclampsia.

Antenatal appointments

If you're healthy and you had no problems with your first pregnancy, then you won't have so many of these. National guidelines recommend you have seven antenatal appointments for a second pregnancy, as opposed to ten for first pregnancies. This may come as a surprise if you had your first baby before 2003 – when it was normal to make fourteen antenatal visits whether there were problems or not. Most people are relieved to go fewer times, but if you're at all worried about anything, you can always make an extra appointment to see your midwife.

If you need or want to take your child to your appointments, don't forget that you often have to wait a long time before you get seen. Take a drink and a snack and something for your child to do so they don't get too restless.

Tiredness

The slightly less wonderful thing about being pregnant for a second time is that because you're older, and because you've got a child to look after already, you're much more likely to feel tired, while at the same time much less likely to get the rest you need. For some reason, when you're pregnant first time around and have no one to look after but yourself (and the dog, plus your partner), friends and family are falling over themselves to make sure you're resting enough, running hot baths for you, buying you chocolates and magazines and making sure you're feeling OK.

Second time around, when you have a small child clinging onto your legs wherever you go – including the loo – and when you could really do with even just ten minutes to sit down, the cosseting and pampering from your partner and other members of the family seem to evaporate. Maybe it's because people have simply forgotten how tiring being pregnant with a small child to look after can be or maybe it's because friends and family know that you're not a novice, they see that you've coped once before and that you're capable as a mother, so forget that you might want help! Whatever the reason, my biggest tip for mothers pregnant with their second child is: don't be afraid to ask for help.

Running around the sofa playing chase with your two year old, plus all the extra things you have to do to look after a child, is tiring enough but added to the fact that your body is working hard to nurture your growing baby it's not surprising that you're exhausted during the day. Friends with similar aged children may be able to take your child with them to the park, to give you a break. And when your partner is around, suggest they take your child out of the house for a bit. If your child is still having a nap in the afternoon, have a rest too. If you can't bring yourself to actually go to bed, then at least sit down with a cup of whatever you can drink without feeling sick and do nothing. It's also important to eat regularly as not eating will make you much more tired. Sleep when your child sleeps if they're still having a nap and, if not, make sure you both have a quiet time where you can sit and read books or watch an episode or two of Peppa Pig. However difficult, it's important to make sure you don't get exhausted, as this can lead to all sorts of problems such as high blood pressure.

Spreading the news

With your first child, you know the excitement of your news will have a big impact. And a lot of people put a considerable amount of thought and creativity into how to spread the news to their friends and family and even to their partners (sending photo frames with pictures of their early ultrasound scan to grandparents-to-be or sending baby bibs with instructions to bring them out in nine months' time, etc.). The very excited will phone up or text everyone they've ever known as soon as they get the positive news including the plumber, who just came to check the boiler last week. Others, more cautious, will wait until the first twelve weeks are over before telling their wider circle of friends, but share knowing winks with their partner as they request a sparkling water at a dinner party or a decaf coffee instead of a double espresso.

There is no reason not to do exactly the same thing you did first time around to spread the news but the truth is the second time around it is not usually such a dramatic story. The novelty has worn off and anyway just as you sit down to make those telephone calls to your friends, your first child suddenly wakes up demanding another hug/drink of water/kiss for Peter the elephant and, by the time you've finally finished, you're so tired you decide to put off the phone calls until tomorrow – and then the next day. I have friends who never got round to spreading the news themselves. They waited until you phoned them about something quite different and then when we'd finished talking about how gorgeous George Clooney was in his latest film, they'd remember their news and casually mention it just as you were going to put the phone down.

The way the news is received and how you are treated may be different this time around too. Parents, in-laws and other relatives may not be quite as excited and enthusiastic as they were the first time and many friends have told me how they felt less important when breaking the news to their parents. A brief 'That's lovely, darling' was about all they got, followed by 'And how's Harry doing at nursery?' You've already provided your parents with their grandchild and, if they're helping out with child care already, they may view the news with a certain amount of concern as to what it will mean for them. Their response may even be one of disapproval – as you detect dark mutterings of 'Are you sure you can cope with two? Shouldn't you have waited longer before having another?'

Telling work

If you're still working for the same company you were with when you had your first child, you'll already know the details of their policy on maternity leave (you won't have to try and find where you put the company handbook and then scratch your head doing calculations and working out what all the different things mean), and you'll have a pretty good idea how your boss and colleagues are likely to respond to the news that you plan to go on leave again. But even if you've got the best and most sympathetic boss in the world, and everything went well first time, your news is not going to be as happy for them as it is for you. So to make it easier for them – and for you – it's worth spending a little time on working a few things out before you break the news to them this time: firstly, do you want to go back to work this time? Full-time or part-time?

You may not know what you want to do until after your baby is born, but if you've definitely decided not to go back to work it's best to give them as much time as possible to find your replacement. If you do want to go back, do you want to take more time off before the baby is born, or less? Do you want to take some extra, unpaid leave? Once you have worked out the answers in your own mind, that's the time to spread the good news, assuming of course your colleagues and boss haven't worked it out already for themselves. Workmates, who see you every day, have an uncanny knack of knowing things about you before you know them yourself and they may well recognize the tell-tale signs of your pregnancy long before you actually tell them the news.

Should I find out the gender?

Almost one of the first questions people ask you about your second pregnancy is whether you want a boy or a girl this time round. And almost every mother will respond, 'I don't mind so long as they're healthy.' But many parents may secretly be longing for their second child to be the opposite sex this time; a girl for mummy, a boy for daddy – the perfectly balanced family. Or they may have other reasons for hoping for a particular gender. Your child on the other hand may more probably and not so secretly be hoping that the baby will be the same sex as them so they can be a real playmate. Does it help to find out beforehand? This is a very personal decision.

The most common reason people give for not wanting to know is that they want it to be a surprise. I was always fairly certain that I was having another boy but I didn't want to actually know and perhaps be disappointed beforehand. I knew that once I held my baby in my arms I wouldn't mind at all, whatever sex it was. For other people, know-ing from the start gives them time to adjust to the news, and being able to tell their first child what they'll be having avoids disappoint-ment at birth. And many people say that while they didn't want to know for their first child, they did for their second. It helps them to know what to buy – whether they'll need new clothes for example if the baby's going to be a different sex. Being able to give the baby a name with certainty and to talk to their child about their baby brother, William, for example was often given as a reason for finding out the second time, too.

Telling your child

Deciding when to break the news to your first child that they are going to have a brother or sister is a much more personal issue. Opinion is divided between those who think that the earlier you tell your child the better so that they have plenty of time to get used to the idea and to prepare for the changes to come, and those who believe that even a day is a long time for a small child, let alone nine months, so it's better to wait until you're at least four or five months pregnant by which time your changing waistline is likely to lead to questions that demand answering.

When you tell your child will partly depend on their age. A very young child, aged under two, is not really going to understand the concept of what you're telling them, especially when there's nothing to see or feel, and so it may be easier to explain when your bump is obviously showing and they can see that something is growing inside your tummy.

Preschool children will be able to understand much better and will be more talkative. For this reason, some people think the best time to tell your child is at the same time as you tell the rest of your friends and family. If you tell your friends and family first, there's always the danger your child will find out from a well-meaning friend congratulating you as you unexpectedly meet them in IKEA. Equally, as most children find it hard to keep a secret – especially one as exciting as having a new baby brother and sister – if you tell them first, they're bound to tell everyone the news anyway.

Although children under five are much more likely to understand the news and be excited about it, their understanding of time may still be shaky. The earlier you tell them, the longer they have to wait for the baby to arrive and some children may get impatient and feel quite fed

Mums on telling their first children:

'We didn't mention my pregnancy to our eighteen month old until I was five or six months along. We decided he wouldn't understand very much any earlier. Also I didn't want to tell him too soon in case something happened, which would confuse him.'

Sarah, mother of George and Ella

'We told our four year old about my pregnancy right away because it takes him a long time to adjust to major changes and I thought he'd need as much time as possible to get used to the idea. I'm really glad we did. We spent a lot of time looking at books about babies and talking about them and preparing him for the changes to come. And by the time our second baby was born he was really excited about being a big brother.'

Jane, mother of Drew and Finn

'We waited until after I'd had the twelve-week ultrasound scan before telling our seven year old the news. I wanted to be as sure as possible that I wouldn't have a miscarriage because at seven years old I think that would have really upset him – more so than for much younger children who don't understand as much. At the same time, I didn't want to wait too long because I wanted to share our excitement with him.'

Charlotte, mother of Josh and Daisy

up and bored. To help them understand the time frame you can make a special baby calendar so they can see that it will be a long time before the baby arrives. Include on it the seasons and the events that will have meaning for them, like going to the seaside in the summer holidays, so it will be clear for example that the baby will arrive after the Easter bunny, and after the hot summer but before their own birthday in the autumn when the leaves fall off the trees.

To help explain to your preschooler about the new baby, get out the photograph album of when they were a baby to show them. Young children always like looking at pictures of themselves so it will be fun for your child as well as a good way of explaining what babies are like and telling them the news.

Older children will have an even greater understanding of the significance of the news. They may also have worked out that something is going on before you plan to tell them. Many parents want to wait until after the first trimester when the greatest risk of miscarriage is over and also when the mother is hopefully beginning to feel more energetic again and less sick before they break the news. Others feel that it is less worrying for an older child to be told the reason why Mummy is feeling tired and being sick. You know your child's temperament best and what is likely to be the most suitable time for them.

How your child will react

However carefully you've prepared it is impossible to predict exactly how your child will react to the news. Some children may be very excited and happy while others may seem more thoughtful and have lots of questions. Be prepared to listen and to answer the questions as reassuringly as you can without giving too much unnecessary information (do think about how you're going to answer those tricky questions about how the baby got in there and how it's going to get out again before you give the news). Depending on the age and interest of the child, some may want to look at a book with you about how babies are made – while others may only want to know if the baby will be a

Liverpool supporter. My eldest son, who was two and a bit when we told him that he'd be having a new brother or sister to look after, was totally underwhelmed and just asked if he could have another biscuit. There seemed little point in going on with the conversation, so we left it at that (and gave him the biscuit).

Dealing with your child's tricky questions about the baby

Deciding what and how to answer your child's questions about where the baby came from and how it gets out is not always easy. I didn't learn how babies were made until my younger sister told me when I was about nine – and I simply refused to believe her! For that simple reason, I think it's better if parents explain these things to their children before they receive the information (or misinformation) from someone else.

But how do you do it? You don't want to scare your child, nor do you want to confuse (lie?) to them about storks and so on. On the whole, most parents feel the best approach is to be honest but many try to keep things as simple as possible. 'When mummies and daddies love each other, they can make a baby', 'A doctor helps to get the baby out in the hospital' or 'Mummies have a special place for the baby to come out' is enough for some children (and parents) to handle. Other parents may feel that their child's question deserves a fuller explanation, using the correct terminology and that if it's explained sensitively and truthfully from a young age, children will accept it without being embarrassed by it. It's up to you what you feel comfortable telling your child and what you feel they will be able to cope with.

Preparing your child before the baby arrives

Once you've broken the news, take the cue from your child as to how much you involve them in your preparations for the new baby. If your child was excited about the news of the new baby, then they will probably enjoy helping you prepare for the baby's arrival; going shopping with you to choose clothes for the baby and helping you to decorate the baby's room. An interested child can come to your antenatal visits and listen to the baby's heart, see the ultrasound scan and feel the baby's kicks, which all will help to make things more real. However, there is no point in dragging a disinterested or angry and resentful child around the shops while you choose new things to buy for a baby that they're not sure they want.

Even if your child is less excited than you'd hoped there are still some things that you can do that may help prepare your child for the changes ahead. Here are some suggestions:

Talk about the baby: don't do this a lot if your child doesn't want to, but don't completely ignore the subject or your child may think they've successfully made the baby go away. When you do mention the baby, refer to them as 'your baby brother or sister' or 'our baby' rather than 'my' or 'the' baby. Talk about their baby as a person. Explain what new babies are like – both the positive and negative things; that to begin with babies sleep a lot and they may cry a lot; that they don't play football for about a year; they don't read you stories; and they're not particularly good at telling jokes either. However, they are very good at listening to your stories, being stroked and, after a few weeks, at smiling and then laughing at your jokes. Emphasizing that babies won't be playmates straight away is, I think, quite important. My son was constantly being told how lucky he was to be getting a new brother or sister to play with, and of course the reality was a huge disappointment. The baby when it finally arrived didn't actually do anything for ages.

Visit real babies: the best way for your child to understand what babies are like is for them to see the real thing – an actual live baby! Go and see friends with new babies and offer to help them so your child can see some of the things that need to be done to look after a baby. It may sink in that this will mean that you'll be busier after your baby is born! If you're planning to breastfeed your baby, you may find that it helps if your child has already seen this happen before so it doesn't seem too odd.

Look at books about babies: go to your local library and have a look at the wide range of picture books and stories there are about babies and children having new brothers and sisters – lots of them deal with jealousy and other emotions that young children feel and this may help your child talk about how they're feeling and realize that it's OK to be feeling upset or angry.

Teach your child how to wait for things: most first children are used to getting help with things the minute they ask for them – the drink of water, the help with putting on shoes, getting out the paints. Saying to your child before the baby is born, 'I will help you as soon as I've finished doing what I'm doing', and making them wait, even just for a short time before they get the help they want, will prepare them for the fact you won't always be able to help immediately with something after the baby is born. Even better, teach your child to be as independent as possible beforehand so they don't need to wait for you. The more your child can do for themselves – play on their own for a while, eat without help, get dressed etc., the easier it will be for both of you.

Establish a bedtime routine: if you haven't got your older child into a bedtime routine yet, or if your child is still waking a lot during the night, you want to try and solve these problems as far as possible before your baby is born. First, because research has shown that children who do not get enough sleep are more likely to suffer all sorts of problems – from being tired and grumpy, to not being able to concentrate during the day and even to being more accident prone. Second, because sleep is just as important for adults and if your child is not getting enough sleep, nor are you, so solving these sleep problems is a number one priority. There are many different methods of solving sleep problems but almost all of them centre around having a good bedtime routine and being consistent about putting your child to bed at the same time each night and allowing your child to fall asleep on their own without the need for you to help them to sleep.

Try to keep big changes to a minimum around the due date

Most small children are conservative; that is they don't like change and are reassured by things being the same. Change makes them feel uncertain and insecure. It's particularly important that you try to make as few changes as possible around the time the baby is due. There will be quite enough changes for your child to get used to after the baby is born. Things like trying to stop your child from using a dummy or encouraging them to give up their night-time bottle, which they find so reassuring, should either be done a long time before the new arrival or otherwise quite a long time afterwards. Comfort objects like dummies and bedtime bottles can often help children in stressful situations so it may be better to let them keep these until the initial settling period is over. Some other big changes to think about well in advance are as follows:

Daycare and nursery school: if your child is old enough, they will love going to nursery school and the normality of the nursery routine can be hugely reassuring for a child who might be unsettled by all the changes at home. Having your child cared for at nursery or daycare will also give you a bit of rest and time alone with your baby. Don't try and send your child to nursery the minute your baby is born though, as they may well think you're trying to get rid of them while you spend more time with the baby. Start them a month or so before – this should be enough time for a child to settle into the routine.

Moving to a big bed: if you're planning to use your child's cot for the new baby then make sure you move your child into a big bed long before the baby is due. Good advice is to put the cot away and then bring it out again for the baby so it's not so apparent that the baby will be sleeping in 'their cot'. If your child doesn't seem ready for a big bed yet, then see if you can borrow a cot for the baby until your child is ready to move.

Toilet training: again, it's not a good idea to try and do this near your baby's due date. For a start, it's not a great time to be running around after your child with a potty when you're heavily pregnant. Secondly, children often regress (start wetting themselves again) after a new baby arrives and this is more likely to happen if the child is only recently toilet trained.

Have fun with your child while it's just the two of you...

I'm not suggesting you disrupt your child's normal routine – or take them out of nursery or daycare. But when you do get to spend time together, think of things you can do which you may not be able to do together for a while. It may be difficult for you to get out and about for a few weeks once the baby's born, so get out now and go to the park for an ice-cream or to the swimming pool. Don't spend your time indoors cleaning the cupboards if your child is just sitting in front of the TV while you do this – go and have some fun doing things you both enjoy together.

...But don't put too much pressure on yourself

Try not to worry too much about making the time you spend with your first child 'perfect'. Beth, mother of Jack and pregnant with her second child, agrees that you want the last few months with your first child to be special, but that this can put on added pressure: 'I took Jack to a café last Friday for a croissant and a hot chocolate as a treat, but the minute we got there Jack grabbed a sugar lump out of the pot on the table. OK I can live with one – but then he wants more, so I had to remove the pot. He started struggling and crying and having a meltdown in the middle of what was a fairly quiet café, and I ended up getting cross and fed up when all I wanted was for it to be really nice. Once the croissant arrived he cheered up and we did have a really nice time but the experience taught me that I should probably lower my expectations and just get on with life rather than trying to make those days "too" special!'

And a final thought from Rosie, mother of Tilly and Fern: 'I wish I hadn't spent so much time while I was pregnant worrying about how Tilly would feel about the arrival of number two and whether she'd be jealous and feel excluded. It's exciting being pregnant and I wish I'd spent more time enjoying it!'

T W O

Happy birth day

You've had nine months to prepare for it, and now the new baby is nearly here. You may find that life with a small child has helped to make the months of pregnancy fly by or you may find that the opposite is true, that being extra tired has slowed things down. But whether suddenly or slowly, you find that your pregnancy is almost over and that the due date is looming. While you want to enjoy your last few weeks as a family of three with only one child to look after – especially if you have just gone on maternity leave and are adjusting to life at home on a daily basis – at the same time you want to get all those things done before the baby is born. You want to have everything ready and organized in time.

Preparing at home

The last thing you may feel like doing when you're heavily pregnant and looking after a child is to add a whole lot more things to your 'To Do' list. So you can ignore this if you like. But I promise you that doing a few practical things before the baby is born will help make life a lot easier afterwards – it's a lot easier to get things done with one child than it is with two!

Food and meals: maybe you've got a partner who's a brilliant cook. Or lots of friendly neighbours who'll come and bring you presents of home-made meals. But if you're the one normally responsible for planning and cooking meals, you don't have any neighbours you've said more than 'Happy Christmas' to and you'd actually like to eat something relatively edible when you come out of hospital, then it's worth preparing a few things so you don't have to cook straight away. Make extra quantities of whatever you're cooking now so you can freeze it, or buy in some ready meals.

For the times that even the thought of taking something out of the freezer and putting it in the oven seems too exhausting, keep a collection of take-away restaurant menus – especially if they deliver. As a back-up they can be a lifesaver!

Shopping: if you haven't got into online supermarket shopping, do it now – it's brilliant! No more pushing around wayward and heavy trolleys, no more embarrassing tantrums when you tell your child they can't have any sweets at the till, no more queuing, no more bending down to unload the trolley, no more feeling guilty you've forgotten to bring your own bags – again; no more lugging heavy bags out of the car and into the house.

With some online supermarkets you can reserve a time for your shopping to be delivered at the same time every week. They'll deliver your usual shopping – unless you edit your list, which you can do up to twenty-four hours beforehand – and bring it into your house. All you have to do is put it away. And although you do have to pay a few pounds for the delivery charge this is usually offset by the fact that you haven't had to pay for petrol to get to the supermarket, or for any of those extra things you put in the trolley on impulse or as a bribe to stop your child from screaming the shop down. So, before the baby arrives, make a start with online shopping, create a list and get to know the system. Remember, you can even get nappies delivered, so it really is a convenient thing to do. And of course, once the baby's born you can add a few treats to the list just for you.

Laundry: you may have forgotten how much extra washing a tiny baby can create – especially if you're using washable nappies. Reorganize your laundry system (if you don't already have one – now's the time to start) and have a separate basket for clean laundry for each child. You can buy very inexpensive laundry baskets, which either stack up or fold away so they don't take up too much space and it makes sorting out the clothes and putting them away a lot easier.

Cleaning: people always tell you not to worry about the housework after you've just had a baby and to just concentrate on your new baby. The thing is that just after you've had a baby is when you get more visitors than ever, including Great Aunt Prudence who's never been to visit before, so it can be hard not to mind if everything has become a tip. Again, maybe your partner will surprise you and manage all the tidying and housework on his own but if you think that's unlikely to happen and more likely to create tension then, if at all possible, try and arrange for someone to come in and do even just a couple of hours a week for the first few months.

Other help: if you've got enough room in your house, arrange for a family member or friend to come and stay with you for a few days after the baby's born. Either to help look after your first child, or the baby, or you! And it can be easier to have someone around to talk to, particularly when your partner has gone back to work.

Childproofing the house: I know you've already childproofed the house for your first child, but as Sarah, mother of four boys, explained to me, it's really important to check that you have done it as thoroughly as possible when you have a second child: 'When you have one, you can look after objects in the house more easily, but when you have two children, one can distract you while the other attempts to eat the glass Christmas tree bauble like an apple (for example!). I did things like put all the breakable things in the kitchen cupboards in an eye-level cupboard and all the baking trays, plastic bowls etc. in the lower ones and the boys used to regularly empty them out and play with them and bash them … and it never mattered. Make full use of socket covers etc., even those behind chairs or where you think they are out of reach!' Depending on the age of your first child, you may have started to relax about certain safety things, but with two children you have to be on your guard all over again. You don't have to fully child-proof everywhere if that's too time consuming, but even if you do just one room that helps. The chances are that you will sometimes need to leave your toddler on their own to play with some toys while you attend to your new baby and it's much easier to relax if you know your child will be safe in the room alone.

A good haircut: this may sound frivolous and vain, but it can make a huge difference to your morale, so it's worth doing. You probably won't have time to get your hair cut for ages after the baby is born, nor will you have time to spend blow-drying and styling your hair (if you ever did). So get a haircut now that needs minimum maintenance – no hair-drying required – but which still makes you look and feel OK instead of frumpy. You will be glad you did – it's better to have a good hair day even when it's a bad hair day.

Packing your hospital bag: with your first baby you probably had your bags packed and ready to go to hospital weeks before the due date. Second time around, you may forget all about such plans until the last minute when your waters break and then find yourself in a panic trying to find the newborn nappies and your favourite cosy blanket. It does-n't take long to do and you will probably remember what to take from last time – what was helpful, what you wished you'd had and what was a complete waste of time. But there is one extra thing you won't have packed last time – a present for the baby to give to their new brother or sister when they meet for the first time. (Although you may not plan for the first meeting to happen in the hospital, it's best to be prepared just in case you need to stay longer than you expect.) This is a popular tip, which really does help make those first introductions easier when your first child meets their new baby. A good idea for a present, for both boys and girls, is a baby doll which can be their very own baby to look after. So go shopping and buy something now.

Arrange some free time: you may not have much free time with one child to look after, but you'll have even less after your second baby is born. Try and arrange to do at least one fun thing just for yourself before the baby is born while you can. This goes for dads too. As Alex, father of Sarah, Leo and Annabel, put it: 'I knew that I'd have no free time ever again after our second baby was born, so the way I prepared beforehand was to play a lot of cricket and golf. There, at least I'm honest! And I was right – I gave up both last season.'

Planning child care while you're having the baby

The most important preparation you can make for going into hospital is planning who will look after your child while you're away. Older children, over three, say, may enjoy having a sleepover at a friend's house, and will see the whole thing as a treat and an adventure. However, unless you're having a Caesarean and know when you're going into hospital, it's a bit much to ask a friend to keep every night for a month free just in case you need to go in. If your labour starts at night, it's also disruptive and possibly alarming for your child to be woken up and bundled into the car and driven to another house to be put back to bed. So have a back-up plan, and keep the number of at least two friends or babysitters you can call in the night to come to your house. Younger children will find it easier being looked after in their own home anyway. Ideally the babysitters or friends will live very close by so that they can get to you quickly. Second labours are often much quicker than the first, so you may not have nearly as much time as you think you will have to get to the hospital, as Nancy discovered when she started to go into labour with her second baby: 'Mum and Dad live three hours away from us and so we arranged that we would call them when I went in to labour and they would start driving (no matter what time of day). This seemed like a perfectly fabulous idea when I was pregnant as my first labour was twenty-four hours … little did I know that my second would be out in five hours from the very first contraction! It all got very scary, my parents tearing through the night and us almost having to call a neighbour round. I got to hospital and had him almost immediately.'

It's also worth planning how you'll manage to look after your child after the contractions have started and before help has arrived. If your child is old enough to understand, and not asleep, it's probably best to warn them what happens – that you might get some pains that take your breath away for a bit but that they'll help to make the baby arrive and that you'll be fine.

If your child has never spent any time away from you, it's a good idea to get them used to the idea of being looked after by whomever you've chosen before you go into the hospital to have the baby. Whether you've chosen grandparents, friends or a babysitter, see if they can come a few times before the baby's born so they can have a look at what your child normally does every day and continue this when you're away.

If he doesn't normally spend a lot of one on one time with your firstborn, it's worth getting your partner to do this too before the baby's due. It will be much easier for them both if they have some practice beforehand. And it will be much easier and more relaxing for you to come back to a house that hasn't been turned upside down as your partner searches cupboards looking for where you keep the Calpol!

The labour

As the weeks go by and the time to go into hospital approaches, the excitement of holding your new baby in your arms may be increasingly tinged with fear and dread of going through labour all over again, especially if you had an unusually long or difficult one the first time. My mother recalls how she'd managed to block out memories of her traumatic labour with me, her first child, until she was being driven into hospital in labour with her second. As the contractions became faster and memories returned she exclaimed, 'Stop! I've changed my mind!'

Dealing with fears

It is not a good idea to leave it until you're going into labour to confront your fears about it or to try and deal with any trauma of your first experience! You will feel much better and more in control if you talk to your midwife about any fears or worries you may have about giving birth this time, before the event. Discuss your first experience with your midwife and tell her what you're finding particularly frightening. Could things have been done differently? If you weren't happy with how the hospital treated you, what are the other choices? Maybe you'd prefer to try a home birth this time? What else would you like to do differently this time? Have you thought about natural forms of pain relief and relaxation techniques? If the experience of your first labour has left you deeply anxious about how you will cope with labour this time, you need to work out a different strategy for managing pain. Visualization and self-hypnosis techniques, which aim to help you release fear and tension, thereby reducing pain, and to achieve a relaxed and positive state of mind are becoming increasingly popular and are particularly recommended for women who have had a previous traumatic birth experience. Get advice on how to avoid the things you're worried about and pain management. Your decisions about what you want for your birth are made easier because you know more about what's involved this time.

Antenatal classes

Lots of mothers think they don't need to go to antenatal or birth preparation classes again and that these are really meant for first timers. But you'd be surprised! Especially if it's a few years since you had your first child, technology moves on at an amazing rate, and things really do change from one pregnancy to the next.

It's worth looking to see if there are any 'refresher' classes in your area, which are designed for second-time mums. Apart from anything else, taking the time out to go to these classes gives you a bit of space to concentrate on your new baby and this pregnancy – something which you may realize you haven't had much time to do while you've been looking after your first child.

Refresher antenatal classes are also a good way of meeting other pregnant mothers who can become an important support network after your baby is born. You may already have this, but if you're new to an area or you find that the timing of your second baby is out of sync with most of your friends' pregnancies, then it's particularly help-ful. The NHS may provide these classes in your area; other private organizations such as the National Childbirth Trust (NCT) do, and these are aimed at second-time mothers, whatever the age gap is since your first child. If you can't find any, then do go to one or two ordinary antenatal classes – if only to remind yourself how to do that controlled breathing.

Easier second time around

Chloe, mother of Oliver and Elise, says, 'Childbirth was easier. Much quicker. I felt much more in control as I knew what was happening and I wasn't worried when I felt like my body was breaking in two!'

The good news is that second labours are on the whole much easier than first ones. In fact, for some mothers like Nancy, the second birth can be positively enjoyable in comparison. 'My first birth was quite frankly brutal and traumatic for lots of different reasons but I think a lot of it was due to my mental state. I felt so out of control and so scared. I had pretty much every intervention and drug possible and was moments away from an emergency C sec. Second time round I felt determined to keep my head throughout the process and relax a bit more. I was so sure I'd want an epidural again and had *no idea* how anyone could consider doing anything less. Albie was born so quickly and the whole experience was just so positive. I didn't even have time for gas and air but I honestly could have done it all again there and then. I just had this incredible hormonal high. It was very, very strange! I just felt amazing and perhaps a little bit smug with myself! I had a TENS machine second time round, which I didn't have the first time, but actually I think it was all to do with my mental attitude and knowing what to expect.'

Mental attitude and knowing what to expect may certainly be part of it, but it also helps that physically you've done this before. Your muscles are used to being stretched so they stretch more easily again this time. Being familiar with what contractions feel like and the stages of labour makes it easier to know what to do and when to do it. It also helps that you've been through the procedure in the hospital, and to really understand what the different types of pain relief can do and whether you want them, though for some people, like Clare, this makes a second labour actually slightly harder. 'I knew how painful it was going to be second time round. You can't kid yourself. You also know that gas and air has only a limited impact.'

Twice as fast

You may find your contractions are more intense this time but this tends to mean that they're working more efficiently too and so, as already mentioned, second labours are usually much shorter, averaging around seven to eight hours instead of fifteen to sixteen hours for first labours. Most women are glad to spend less time in labour, though in some cases it can be so quick as to be alarming, as Emma, who was having a home birth, discovered: 'I went into labour at 8.30pm and Molly made her entry into the world at 10.22pm – just twenty minutes after the midwives arrived. Waiting for the midwives – who weren't responding to their pagers – was stressful and I spent the last hour desperately searching for the section on how to deliver your own baby in the *What to Expect when you're Expecting* book!'

So, if you're planning to have your baby in hospital, don't leave it until the last minute to go in, especially if it's rush hour. No one really wants to give birth in a car.

More experienced partner

As well as looking forward to shorter labours, you also have a partner (assuming you have the same one) who has been through this before. He will probably have learned not to be shocked by your knowledge of swear words (or at least not to show you how shocked he is) and will be more likely to know what to do that really helps, rather than standing around awkwardly mopping your forehead with a wet flannel or, worse, sitting in the chair reading *Auto Trader* while eating your store of energy-providing glucose drops.

You too will know more what you want your partner to do, and you may find it helps to talk about this with him. Work out beforehand what support you want him to give you this time and what things did and did not help last time.

A bigger baby?

For some reason second babies tend to be bigger than first ones but on average only by about 138 grams (5 ounces) – so don't panic! This doesn't mean that you're going to have a horrendous birth. First, although your baby may be heavier than last time, it is unlikely that the head will be that much bigger – which is the important bit as far as giving birth is concerned.

Also, if your first baby weighed over 3.72 kilograms (8.3 pounds), you are actually likely to have a lighter baby second time around.

Episiotomies and tears

Because second labours are usually easier and quicker, the chances of needing an episiotomy and stitches or tearing are also reduced. So, if this happened to you first time around, this does not mean you will necessarily have to go through it again – and the scar from the first time doesn't need to tear again either. To help prevent it from happening again (and in my opinion anything is worth trying to prevent it), the recommended advice is perineal massage beforehand, and to try and use an upright position for pushing in the second stage of labour. Recovering from stitches is bad enough with just one baby to look after, when you can sit or lie down most of the time.

Having a Caesarean

If you had a normal birth the first time, it doesn't necessarily follow that you will the second time. You may develop a condition such as placenta previa or your baby may be breech which means that it may not be considered safe for you to deliver vaginally. For many women who have had a particularly traumatic labour the first time, an elective Caesarean birth second time around is preferable to the prospect of a repeat trauma with another vaginal birth. Although you may be disappointed, there are certainly advantages if you are having an elective Caesarean (as opposed to an emergency Caesarean, which may also happen second time around and where the only advantage is that your baby survives):

*   Planning is much easier because you know exactly when you will be going into hospital.
*   You can make arrangements for your child to be looked after with certainty and be able to prepare your child by explaining when you will be going to hospital, and probably how long for.
*   The birth itself is quick and can feel very peaceful as your baby is quickly brought into the world without any trauma.

But do be prepared. Many women say that they hadn't really taken on board that having a Caesarean is major abdominal surgery and were not expecting it to be so painful for so long afterwards. Make sure that you have arranged plenty of child care to help you when you get back home afterwards. Some women say that it takes months to feel fully recovered.

Having a VBAC (vaginal birth after Caesarean)

About 30 per cent of women who had a Caesarean first time around decide to try and give birth vaginally the second time around and do so successfully. Whether or not you can do this will depend on the reason you had a Caesarean in the first place. If it was an emergency operation because your baby was in distress, for example, then the chances of that happening again are much lower, and you may have no problems with a vaginal birth. If it was because of an existing condition that you have, such as diabetes, or your pelvis is too small, then you will need to have a second Caesarean delivery.

Many women feel very strongly that they want the chance to give birth vaginally. They believe it will help them to feel more connected and to bond better with their baby, and that it is part of the ritual of motherhood. Here are what a few women had to say about their experience:

Mums on trying for a VBAC:

'I was very nervous about trying for a vaginal birth after having a Caesarean with my daughter. I didn't know whether I'd be able to cope with the pain or whether I'd be able to do it – and dreaded ending

up having to have surgery anyway. But I really wanted to try. We knew this would be our last child and my last chance to give birth.'

Melissa, mother of Nina and Florence

'Deciding to try for a VBAC was the best decision I've ever made. Even though I did have tearing and it was uncomfortable, I enjoyed it – and the feeling of success and achievement at the end was incredible – I don't think I'll ever come down from that high. Recovering after the VBAC was a million times better than my recovery from the Caesarean; the difference was immeasurable.'

Cathy, mother of Nathan and Silvie

As well as the emotional reasons, there are practical advantages to a vaginal birth too – particularly second time around. Although the birth itself may be (will definitely be) more painful, your recovery time is *much* quicker and the chances of infection are less too. Breastfeeding and life at home with two children will be easier if you haven't had major surgery.

Having a home birth

Deciding to give birth at home is still far from common nowadays – about one in fifty women choose to do so, according to government statistics. However, more mothers choose to do this second time around, either because they feel more confident about childbirth generally or possibly because they wish to avoid repeating an unhappy hospital experience. Women who have chosen to have their babies born at home generally report feeling much more relaxed and in control of what was happening to their bodies and the birth. The evidence also suggests that there is less instrumental interference in home births and that those babies who are born at home score higher in their APGAR tests – the tests taken immediately after your baby is born to check how well they are doing.

The other deciding factor for many women second time round is that they want their first child to feel more involved in the birth of the baby. According to family health visitor and former midwife Ruth Fromow, who has been present at a number of home births, it works very well for many mothers. So long as there is someone on hand to occupy and look after the first child when necessary, it can be a very positive experience, which strengthens the family and makes the child feel very involved.

Every woman has a different reason for choosing the type of birth they want. Here is Emma's story of her experiences of having a home birth: 'Strangely, I had never considered anything other than a home birth for both my first and second pregnancies. When I look back now my innate fear of hospitals won over any possible considerations about the risks of a home birth, but I'm glad – it was absolutely the right decision for me. Both births took place in a birthing pool situated between the cooker and the washing machine – a sign of things to come! My only worry about the second home birth was that the baby would arrive when I was on my own with my eldest daughter but after drafting assurances that friends and family would rally round and take care of Daisy, I put that to the back of my mind and left things in the hands of fate. But thankfully it all ended well and, within moments of her birth, Molly was feeding and resting in her own home, content and secure and surrounded by her family. I wouldn't have wished for it any other way and am so grateful that both my daughters were able to enjoy such a peaceful introduction to life.'

Provided you are a low-risk mother, and it is not thought probable that you should have any complications in childbirth, you may find that a home birth is the right choice for you too.

Be prepared for the unexpected

Of course, while many second births are easier, this can't be guaranteed, nor can you be sure that you will end up with the birth you have planned. You may know from your first experience of giving birth that no matter how detailed your birth plan or how well you have prepared beforehand, things don't always go as you hope they will. And this is just as true for a second baby, as Nicola remembers when her second son, Thomas, was born: 'I was struck with the dreaded pre-eclampsia at thirty-five weeks. It was at this stage I was just beginning to start thinking about a plan for introducing the new baby to my nearly two-year-old Freddie. All that went out the window. I ended up leaving for hospital in the middle of the night and not returning for four weeks. Not exactly what I dreamed of for Freddie's introduction to his brother ... Looking back I am surprised that I did not feel guilty about leaving Freddie to get on with life, but to be honest I did not. Thomas was prem, in special care and at certain stages fighting for life itself. I was totally exhausted, recovering from a C section and emotionally challenged shall we say! There simply was no room for Freddie. During this time Tim (my husband) formed an incredibly close relationship with Freddie – they survived the storm together. I also leant heavily on my loving and supportive family who relished the opportunity of being able to offer practical help, when they could do so little for Thomas in his incubator. It makes me laugh looking back; we plan parts of our lives so carefully then reality happens. But we all got through and I don't think we are too emotionally scarred.'

It's impossible to be prepared for any eventuality, but accepting that second births can be just as unpredictable as first ones may lessen the shock if things don't happen as you expected.

After the birth

How you feel

Physically: if you've had an easier birth, with no stitches or tears, you are of course much more likely to feel better physically this time. After-pains come as a nasty surprise though. These are the pains you get when your uterus contracts as you breastfeed your baby, which you may not have been aware of at all with your first child. These are much stronger and can be incredibly painful after you've had your second baby. You may need to ask the nurse for something stronger than the over-the-counter pain relief tablets you normally take.

Emotionally: you may feel better emotionally immediately after your second child is born, too. After being in labour through the whole night with my first son, an epidural, forceps, an episiotomy and stitches, I was pretty tired when he at last arrived. I was also dazed, shocked and overwhelmed with emotions and by the sudden realization of our responsibility towards this new life we had created. Over the next two days in hospital I can remember constantly thinking to myself 'Am I doing this right?', 'Is this what you are supposed to do?', and looking with admiration at the experienced mums who so naturally and so easily held their babies in their arms and fed them.

When my second son was born, everything worked like a dream. Contractions started after lunch and, without any intervention or pain relief, by 7 o'clock in the evening I lay propped up in bed looking at my newborn son snuggled into my shoulder thinking I knew exactly what to do. It wasn't scary. I had become one of those experienced mums who knew how to look after a baby – how to dress him without fear of pulling his arms off, how to change his nappy in my lap, how to lift him up without startling him. The realization was deeply satisfying and I felt on top of the world.

Feeling different this time

Once your second child is born, mothers often feel a mixture of emotions. Not everybody feels elated immediately. Guilt, an emotion which seems to come attached to motherhood, can come creeping in almost the moment your second child takes their first breath. Some feel guilty if this time doesn't feel quite as intense – neither so shocking nor so joyous – as it did the first time; some mothers feel guilt towards their elder child for the changes that will happen with a new baby at home; others can feel guilty for falling in love with their new baby and wanting to spend all their time with them. Anxiety about how to cope looking after two is a common feeling too.

It is quite normal to feel this seesaw of emotions after giving birth – weepy one minute, full of love and joy the next. Try not to make comparisons and, if at all possible, try to accept your feelings and not be too worried by them. It's important to remember that your hormones are all over the place in the first few days after giving birth and it takes time for them to settle down. It takes time for your body to start recovering too, and for you to adjust to the idea of being a mother of two.

Your child at home

For my husband, the big difference about having our second baby was that this time he did not – could not – stay with me for long. Unlike the first time where we both stared for hours at our newborn baby with thoughts for nothing and no one else, we now had another child to think of. We had a child at home who, although probably asleep by now, we didn't want to leave for long in case he woke up and neither of us was there. I think for this reason the reality of being parents to two children hit my husband before it did me. We had two children to look after now and my husband had to go home to look after our eldest – for the first time on his own. This was the beginning of a new family life.

How long to stay in hospital

These days you may not have much choice about how long you can stay in hospital. If you had an uncomplicated delivery, and you and the baby are fine, as a second time round mum, you may be surprised to find that you are encouraged to leave much earlier than you did before, as soon as all the routine checks have been completed – which may be very soon indeed. You could find yourself walking (or sort of hobbling) out of the hospital with your baby within six hours of having given birth.

And for some mums, like Annie, mother of Lily and Sam, that is exactly what they want to do: 'I couldn't wait to get home. I've never liked hospitals anyway and I simply couldn't see the point in staying. I didn't need to be shown how to do anything, like breastfeeding and actually I found it harder to do in the ward with other people's visitors constantly coming and going. But mostly I just wanted to get home to be with my eldest child, Lily. I didn't know whether she was missing me but I was certainly missing her and it didn't feel right that I should only be with the baby.'

If you are given the opportunity to stay for longer, however, then many mums recommend this. As Sarah, mother of James and Will, told me: 'I wanted to stay in hospital for as long as I could. Even though having Will was quicker and easier than having my first child,

I knew I wasn't up to facing the reality of home life too soon. While you are in hospital there are no meals to prepare, no laundry to do, no housework to feel guilty about, in fact nothing to do except to look after your baby – just as you did with your first. You need to have that time where you are being looked after by professionals and to gather the strength to be a mother of two. I simply refused to go home!'

Should your child visit you and the baby in hospital?

The general advice is that the sooner you introduce your child to their new sibling the better it will be, but some people feel that a hospital is not the right place for their child to meet their new baby. They also want to have just a bit of time with their new baby alone. There are a few other things that need to be taken into account too:

The age/temperament of your child: if you have a very young child who may get upset at not being able to stay with you in the hospital and not understand why you aren't coming home with them, then you might want to think about how you will manage this. Some children are able to manage being separated from you while they are happily being looked after at home by friends and family, but the minute they see you they go to pieces. They are unable to cope with hospital visits where they have to go through the pain of separation all over again. If you decide it is still best for your child to see you, make sure they know what will happen before they come. See how they manage and if they get upset or tired, don't make the visit too long.

How long you will be in hospital: if you are only planning to stay in the hospital for a few hours, you may prefer not to disrupt your child's routine by bringing them into the hospital. However, some experts agree that bringing home the new baby together as a family can be beneficial. Your partner can bring your child in to collect you and bring you and the baby home. However, if you are having a Caesarean birth and know that you will be in the hospital for four or five days then your child will definitely want to visit.

The health of your child: if your child has recently been exposed to chicken pox or another infectious disease you will want to keep them away from the maternity ward as well as your own new baby.

Introducing your child to their new brother or sister

The first time your elder child meets their new baby is an important moment – for you anyway, whether it's in the hospital or at home. We probably all have a sentimental picture in our head of how we'd like our elder child to greet their new baby brother or sister: with tender smiles and a kiss planted lovingly on the baby's forehead, while you look on proudly and serenely at this gentle scene. This may actually happen, but don't be surprised if it's not quite like that. Just as you may be feeling a mixture of emotions, so may your child. They may not want to look at the baby, let alone say something nice about it or stroke it. They may not even want to look at you if they are feeling abandoned by you, and only cling to Dad. Or your attention may be the only thing they really want right now.

Emma remembers vividly the moment her daughter met her new sister for the first time: 'I had a home birth which was lovely and quick and all happened while my daughter was asleep. When she woke up in the morning she came into my room, completely unsuspecting, and there was the new baby. She didn't say anything, but I could tell she was furious. The look in her eyes gave it away – she was not happy at all.'

It's important to remember that however much you want the first visit to go well, it isn't the end of the world if it doesn't. How they get on at that first meeting is not an indication of what things will be like in the future. But of course you want it to be a happy occasion, so here are some suggestions to make the first meeting easier:

* Make sure the first meeting is a quiet meeting without any other visitors present. Your child may be overwhelmed if too many other grandparents, aunts and uncles are all there watching how they react. Instead of it being a natural first meeting, your child may feel simply shy and self-conscious.

* Try and arrange for your baby to be in the cot when your child first arrives so you can give the child hugs and kisses and lots of attention. Make a great fuss of them. If the first thing they see is you holding the baby and unable to hold them, this may understandably create feelings of jealousy.

* If the first meeting will be when you bring the baby home from the hospital, then some people suggest that it is better if your child is out when you first arrive home. You can then do everything that needs to be done for the baby and yourself, so that you are quite ready to give all your attention to your child when they come in.

* Give your child time to choose when they are ready to look into the cot to see the baby. And don't force them to make comments about their baby until they volunteer them. If the comments are not quite as positive as you had hoped, try not to be upset – it doesn't mean that your children will never like each other. Your older child just needs a bit of time.

* Don't forget the present you bought for the baby to give their big brother or sister. This is not bribery – just a practical way of helping to make your child feel more positive towards their new baby by associating them with the pleasure of having a new toy. As Chloe remembers after their daughter was born: 'We

sneaked the baby in and put her into her crib. Next to her, we lay a wrapped up fire engine for our son. We brought our son in and introduced him to his sister and then said the present was from her. He loved it. He wanted to touch Elise but he was mostly interested in his new fire engine.' Another advantage of a new toy is that it gives your firstborn something to play with when you're busy with the baby.

* If your firstborn is excited about meeting their new baby, they might enjoy choosing a 'birthday' present with Dad to give to the baby.

* If your child wants to hold the baby with you, let them. They can sit with you on your lap while you hold the baby together – a special moment indeed.

THREE

The first weeks
at home with two

The waiting and the anxiety of the labour and birth is over, the person you've been waiting to meet for the last nine months is in your arms, and now it's time to go home. What will it be like this time? The probability is that you'll feel a mixture of things as you make your way through the hospital corridors following the signs marked 'Exit'. These feelings might range from 'Oh, crikey, I'm sore', especially if you're coming home just hours after giving birth, to excitement, joy, pride and infatuated love for your new baby. Then as you get into the car and strap your baby into their car seat, the nerves may start to kick in – will your child like their new sibling? Then, just as you get to your front door, full-scale panic might overwhelm you as you realize that this is it, you've got two children now, and somehow you've got to manage to look after them both.

There's no knowing what the first few weeks will be like for you. Everyone's first few weeks at home will be different depending on the temperament and health of your baby and how well they feed and sleep, the reaction of your toddler to their sibling, and the level of help and support you get from your partner, family and friends.

For some mothers, like Susie, these first few days at home are suffused with a sort of golden glow: 'I was really looking forward to seeing Ella (my eldest) and introducing her to her new brother. Ella was so sweet with him, wanting to show him where he'd be sleeping and the rest of the house. The tour of the house ended up in our bedroom and we all ended up getting into the big bed – all four of us – and watching a movie. I can remember looking at the two of them – my two children – and thinking that it was the happiest day of my life. And the first few weeks carried on like that really, while David was at home anyway, a glorified holiday.'

While for some the first few days or even weeks can be like a wonderful honeymoon and live up to all their idealized expectations, many mothers find this lasts only for as long as their partner is at home all day to help, or other kindly friends and relatives, and before the novelty of the baby wears off for their elder child. This was certainly true for Nancy: 'For the first two weeks I was on this ridiculous high, I had this huge hormonal rush, and there were loads of people on hand to help. Stan loved all the attention and Albie was such a good little baby. Life was just perfect at first. But gradually, as all the visitors left and my husband went back to work things just got really hard.'

Clare had a similar experience: 'The first week was bliss as I had a full-time Norland nanny to look after Isabelle, and Grace slept the whole of her first week. The result was I had time to read Barbara Kingsolver's *Poisonwood Bible*, which was brilliant. And I thought what a great baby she was as the first had been full on from the word go. Then all hell broke loose as I tried to go it alone with two babies at very different stages of their development. I just remember being exhausted.'

For others, things are hard right from the start and pass in a blur of tiredness and exhaustion, in hours of endless feeding, of getting up in the middle of the night, of trying and failing to stay calm and on top of things, and of going overboard to give attention to their first child (and pretending not to mind when they tell you they don't want you to read a book to them, they want Daddy). 'The first weeks at home were dreadful,' remembers Vicci. 'Oscar had colic and reflux [when the baby's stomach contents come back up into their food pipe or mouth due to a weak valve at the end of the food pipe, which is meant to keep the food down] so I was exhausted and bad tempered with Olivia. In turn Olivia took to pinching Oscar to make him upset as she was so jealous.'

The reality of life with two children

No matter how lovely your new baby is, sleeping for the textbook sixteen hours a day; and however adorable and sweet-tempered your first child, the fact is that looking after two children is more work and more tiring than looking after one. There is usually a moment when the reality of this suddenly hits you. It might be in the delivery room, when your new baby is put into your arms, it might be the moment you see your first child after you've had your baby, it might be the first day you get home, or not until a few days later when all the visitors have come and gone and your partner has returned to work.

For me it was about a week after I'd got home from hospital with Rory, my second son. My mother-in-law had gone home back to Norfolk and my husband was away, so it was the first time I was really on my own with the two boys. Although it was late October it was a beautiful day and Harry wanted to play football outside – with me as goal-keeper. OK, I wasn't sure I'd be throwing myself at the ball to save too many goals (I didn't feel I'd recovered that quickly from the birth), but the baby was asleep, so this was the perfect time to show that I could do brilliant mothering and give my first child the attention he needed. But first of all we had to get outside. And by the time I'd got Harry to put on his trainers instead of his flip-flops, persuaded him that yes he did have to wear a coat or at least a jumper over his T-shirt, then tried to find his Liverpool scarf at the bottom of the washing basket because the other red one was too itchy, Rory woke up. And by the time I'd changed him, got him dressed and into his winter snowsuit, and into the pram, he had started to cry. I looked at my watch and realized that he was probably hungry. Harry was looking at me accusingly – was I going to play football or not? And I wanted to cry too. How on earth did you do it? What do you do when both your children need you at the same time? How was I going to manage looking after my new baby and my elder child who right now needed more attention, not less, than ever before? How was I going to cope with twice the work when there was still only one of me – and a tired me at that?

No amount of preparing beforehand can change the fact that there will be times when the sheer weight of responsibility of looking after two children can feel overwhelming. Especially in those first few weeks after coming home when you're still recovering from the birth, your baby is feeding every few hours and you don't know whether it's day or night, and your first child is adjusting to having to share you and you just want to go Aaagghh. But perhaps it does help to know that almost every mother of two will at some point or other be feeling the same thing and that most mothers find the first few weeks at home difficult at times, especially if they don't have help and both children are at home all day long. It may help to know too that there are things you can do to make life in the first few weeks easier, both for you and your partner, for your elder child and for the baby.

Looking after your baby – what will be different?

You're a more confident mum

The huge difference and one of the most positive things about the first few weeks with your new baby is that it's much less nerve-racking than the first time – you know what you're doing. You've looked after a newborn baby before, you know how to change a nappy, how to soothe a crying baby, how to feed them, how to hold them and dress them. It doesn't take you all morning to work out how to do the poppers on the babygro and you don't have to screw up all your courage to give them a bath – you know you can hold your baby in the bathwater without drowning them and you don't have to creep into your baby's room every ten minutes after you've put them down to sleep to check that they're still breathing (although you may still find yourself doing this). You are not nearly so anxious about your ability to care for your new baby and so you are much more likely to enjoy them. In short, many women feel more confident. It's always more fun doing something when you know what you're doing and when you feel you're quite good at it. As Jo remembers: 'When Alex, my first child, was born, I was so nervous leaving the hospital – it seemed amazing that I was allowed to take him home without having passed any qualifications and with no experience at all with babies and I was terrified I'd do something wrong and hurt him. He was so precious. I think it took me a whole hour to change his nappy the first time and I did spend a lot of time worrying. By the time James was born all that side of things was really easy. I felt that I was much better at being a mother of a baby. I really enjoyed that.'

Not all babies are the same

Mums on the differences between first and second babies:

'I was completely unprepared for how different my second daughter would be from my first. Sometimes I felt like a first-time mother all over again.'

Caroline, mother of Franny and Issy

'If I'm honest, I'd been dreading the first few weeks with our new baby because I thought she'd be exactly the same as her elder sister had been. In fact, I'd nearly decided not to have a second child because of that. Tamsin never slept, she cried the minute I'd try to put her down and trying to feed her was a nightmare – we later discovered that she had reflux and that was probably why she seemed so angry all the time. But Hannah was just totally different. She was calm and contented – I didn't realize it could be like that.'

Sally, mother of Tamsin and Hannah

Having said that you'll feel more confident because you've looked after a baby before, you may quickly discover that having looked after one baby doesn't make you an expert on all babies. You may find that looking after your second baby is a completely different experience – and not just because you've also got an older child to look after.

Babies are not all the same and one of the biggest surprises for many mothers is how very different their two children can be. You may have a different sex baby this time – and even routine care of a baby boy is different from a baby girl (how to clean their bottoms, and put their nappies on for example – with a boy you need to watch out for them peeing in the air and with a girl remember to wipe from front to back). Tricks that you learned with your first child may not work at all for your second baby. Your first baby may have loved to be held tight and hugged close; your second baby may resist it. Your first baby may have taken to a dummy straight away and been soothed by sucking it, but your second baby may spit it out and only be content when feeding from you.

Often second babies are thought to be easier to look after than first babies, though whether this is because of the baby's temperament or because of the mother's ability is debatable, but while some second babies may be more laid back, this is not always the case. It can be particularly surprising if your first child was an easy, placid baby, who settled quickly and happily into a routine, and your second child does not. If you've never had to deal with a baby who seems to cry whatever you do, or a baby who doesn't feed well, or who never sleeps for longer than a few minutes at a time (or so it seems), then it can almost feel like you're a first-time mum, a complete novice. Which, in a way, you are. It is the first time you have been a mother to this particular child. You will have new and different experiences with your second child which you didn't have with your first, as well as familiar ones. This is your very first second child, a unique individual with their very own set of needs and requirements.

Combined care

The other big difference about looking after your new baby is that with a toddler to look after as well, you will have less time to spend exclusively with your baby. Many of the things you do for your baby during the day you will be doing with your older child in tow. Your baby will be used to more noise and more company right from the start – used to having a small face peering at them intently with varying degrees of affection, used to having small hands grasp theirs, used to the alternate shouts of delight and frustration that your toddler fills the house with, used to being held by you while you are busy doing something else. On the whole this is not a bad thing for your baby – babies can sleep with noise going on around them and having an older brother or sister will probably make them more sociable.

It will be different for you, though, and you may find that it takes a bit of time to learn how to do two things at the same time. You will find that you learn how to feed your baby while making a brick tower for your toddler, how to change your baby's nappy with a small child tugging at your jumper, how to put your baby down for a sleep while singing nursery rhymes for your toddler. You will learn how to care for your baby more efficiently and in less time than you did with your firstborn.

Survival tips for looking after your baby

Don't be surprised at how different your second baby is from your first: he or she may be easier or more difficult to look after than your first child. Be prepared to try different ways of caring for this baby. **Ask your health visitor for help and advice:** friends and family tend not to be as forthcoming with advice and suggestions as before (for which you may be thankful), but even community midwives and health visitors will sometimes assume that a second-time mum needs less help than a first-time one in the business of caring for their baby. Don't be shy about asking – there's no reason why you should know everything about babies. You have just as much right and need to ask for help as a novice first-time mum.

Change your newborn's nappies on the floor: even if you've got a wonderful waist-level changing station to make changing your baby's nappy easier on your back, it's safer to change your newborn on the floor in case you suddenly have to rush to the aid of your toddler.

Try using a sling: to help with multi-tasking you will find that using a sling is a life saver. You can keep your baby close to you all the time, give them the comfort and warmth they need – and sometimes feed them too – while having your hands free to play with your toddler, turn the pages of a book, put the dishes away, lay the table, etc.

Accept help: make the most of any help you receive in the early weeks to spend some time alone with your baby, to give them your exclusive attention and to get to know them (remembering you will also need to spend time alone with your older child). Enjoy the night-time feeds and time alone with your baby while your toddler is asleep.

Don't withhold affection from your baby for fear of upsetting your older child: your older child may feel jealous, for a while anyway, but it is more important that your baby should be loved with as much tactile affection as you give your first child.

Prioritize: you can't do everything and you may not be able to do as many things with your second baby as you did with your first. The trick is to prioritize. Your newborn's essential needs come first. Provided that you give them food, warmth and comfort they will be fine. It doesn't matter if they wear the same babygro two days in a row, or if they don't have a bath for several days. They will survive.

Don't leave your baby to cry for too long because you are doing something with your toddler: as a second-time mum you will be less anxious to rush to your baby at the first whimper, and more quickly able to distinguish what your baby's different crying sounds mean. And that is fine. But responding as quickly as you can to your baby's urgent cry is important.

Looking after your elder child

The ease of your first few weeks at home will depend a great deal on how well your older child adapts to life with the new baby. The arrival of a sibling is a massive event in their life and one that you hope will be a very happy one, but for some children it may not be that happy to begin with. It may seem to your child as if everything in their world has taken a turn for the worse. To begin with, there is the constant stream of visitors coming, not to see them, but to see the new baby. Some of their favourite people may be visiting, but even if Grandma plays with them a bit, she's not exclusively interested in them anymore. Then there's Dad who may be around a lot more and that's great but he, too, spends some time hugging and kissing another child that is not them. And as for Mum, she's always tired, doesn't have nearly as much time for them as before and if she starts playing a game, you can bet your bottom dollar that she won't finish it because she'll be picking up the baby and feeding it. Nothing seems the same any more. A child who feels like this will need a lot of time and attention, reassurance and love from you and your partner.

But perhaps your child will take the arrival of a sibling completely in their stride. And certainly the first few weeks, while the baby sleeps a lot and isn't mobile, can be the easiest for any older child.

However your child reacts, you want to do what you can to make your child feel secure and loved and to minimize the potential for jealousy both in the early days and later on. So how can you help your child to adjust? Here are some suggestions to help your child adjust in the first few weeks:

Limit visitors in the early days: some parents decide to ban visitors for the first few days to allow themselves time to settle down as a family and to adjust to the new pattern of life with a new baby. Having two children to give your attention to, some people feel, is quite enough without also having to give your attention to anyone else. Not having any visitors for a few days means you don't need to worry about how you look or about whether you're still in your pyjamas at lunchtime, you don't need to think about the state of the house, or whether you've got enough teabags to go round and you can focus all your time on doing just what you and your children need and want. On top of that, visitors who are less sensitive to the needs of your firstborn and who come rushing in with presents for the new baby can make life quite a lot worse.

Let visitors help: on the other hand, you do of course want to see your friends and family and to show them the new addition to the family. At some time or other, you also want to have contact with the outside world again. Visitors can be enormously helpful too, so long as they don't spend too much time cooing over the baby, don't expect to be entertained and have actually come to help you. Tactful and sensitive visitors can help to make your firstborn child feel just as special, if not more so, than the new baby. Your elder child will love it if they are made a big fuss of first and probably won't mind at all that the baby is given a present if they are given one too for being such a great 'big brother or sister'. They may enjoy showing the visitor all the things they've done at nursery school, the lovely picture they've just drawn and the new presents they've just got – oh, and their new baby too. Lots of children will enjoy the celebratory atmosphere if they feel a part of the reason for the celebration.

Some people warn their visitors in advance to make sure they pay attention to their elder child and request that if any presents are being given to the baby, one could be brought for the older child too. If you feel this is a bit presumptuous, a handy tip is to keep a supply of small presents ready that you can give your elder child on such occasions so they don't feel left out.

Give your child special time and attention

This is really important. What your child needs more than anything is to know that they aren't being abandoned for the latest model and that you still love them – spending one-to-one time with them, as well as ensuring they are not ignored when you are with the baby, is how you do it. This is easier said than done, I know, if you have a fretful baby whose feeding and sleeping schedule is erratic. If your partner is around he can help either by spending some time with the baby so you can be with your child, or by giving your child special attention while you concentrate on getting the baby settled and into a vague sort of routine. If you do not have a partner, or they are not on hand to help, you may need to get a friend, relative or babysitter to come and help so you and your older child can do something together – just the two of you like it used to be. Going out without the baby, even for just a quarter of an hour, can help both of you – especially if you've been stuck in the house for most of the day.

● *Use the time while your baby is asleep to be with your toddler*
If you're lucky you will have a baby who sleeps a lot in the first few weeks, so in fact you may have more time than you think to spend with your older child. Try to use the time while your baby is asleep to do things with your older child, rather than doing chores around the house. It doesn't matter what you do, so long as it's something your child enjoys and you do it together.

You may be feeling exhausted and need to do something restful, so read books together in bed or watch a DVD – later on you can do more energetic things with them.

Looking at photograph albums of when your child was a baby is also a good thing to do – as it not only helps a very young child understand that the baby won't always be a baby and may be more of a playmate later on, but also helps them see that they were once just like their new brother/sister, being given the same attention and so they haven't missed out.

- *Give your child attention at the same time as the baby*

Chloe explains: 'I worried a lot about being able to entertain Oliver whilst having to look after Elise and I still do a bit, but I try and make time when I put Elise down (in the same room) and read a book to Oliver, so he's getting all my attention.'

This is where the meaning of multi-tasking really becomes apparent. Both your children need you at the same time, and somehow you have to manage to do not just two things at once, but a whole host of things.

Feeding time: if you find that you are spending a lot of time feeding your baby, think of things you can do with your child while you're feeding. Some mothers have a basket of special toys and books that are brought out only for looking at while the baby is feeding. Sit on the floor while you're feeding, so you're at the same level as your first child, and play a game or do a puzzle together.

Let your child help you look after the baby: not only does this mean your child can spend more time with you but it is one of the best things you can do to build a positive relationship between your children and minimize pangs of jealousy. It may help your older child feel proud and important too. If your child isn't interested, don't make them spend time with the baby, but lots of children will actually want to help you. They can help the baby open the presents in the first few days and they can take photos of the baby. They can get the nappy and spread it out, or choose what clothes the baby will wear today, get the towel at bath-time and find a toy to put in their cot at bedtime. They can amuse the baby by singing to it and holding their hand and smiling at the baby – the reward when the baby smiles back will be huge! If you tell them that the baby is smiling at them because the baby likes them, your child is bound to feel pleased and proud.

Talk to your child about what you're doing with the baby: talk to your child about the baby and explain why it's crying and what it needs. You can show them the baby's soft spots (I remember being fascinated and slightly horrified by these as a child) and the umbilical cord – though again I know some children who found the sight of this very upsetting and the parents had to be careful to wait until after the stump had dropped off before letting their child help at bath-time! Tell them what they were like when they were a baby and how you cared for them.

Let your child hold the baby: of course you have the mother's natural instinct to protect your baby and watching your first child trying to pick up the baby can be alarming, but try not to panic! Babies are very robust and if you overreact whenever your toddler is a little bit rough, you run the risk of alienating your child. Constantly urging your child to 'be careful!', or shouting 'Not like that! Gently!' does nothing for your nerves or their self-esteem either. So teach your child how to handle the baby carefully. Depending on how old they are you can either hold the baby together or have rules about how to do it: 'Always ask a grown-up first, and never pick up the baby on your own. Sit down – on a cushion on the floor is probably safest – and wait for the grown-up to give you the baby. Tell a grown-up when you've had enough and don't just stand up and let go!' Your child will model their parenting skills on you. Showing them how to be gentle with the baby, and how to be loving and caring will not only be better for the baby, but help your firstborn too.

What about when you're playing a game with your child and your baby cries? Some people recommend that leaving your baby to cry for a little until you've finished the game will demonstrate to your firstborn that the baby doesn't always come first. So long as it is for a very short time and only occasionally, this may work. But it can be reassuring for your child to know that you are not ignoring the baby's needs in order to satisfy them. They need to know that you will look after both of them. If you withhold affection from the baby, you may actually be making your older child more insecure and anxious, not less. The child may fear that if you can delay tending to a permanent member of the family, maybe one day you will do the same to them. Displays of affection are helpful to everyone in the family.

Praise your child

Don't forget to tell your child how much you love them and how special they are to you – it will make a difference to how your child feels. This may seem obvious, but it can be easy to forget to actually say it. Praise them for all the good things they do (be specific) and any kindness they show to the baby. Tell them how proud you are of them and tell other people too within earshot of your child.

Try and stick to your child's normal routine

Chloe, mother of Oliver and Elise, talks about routines: 'I thought, at the beginning, that I would never manage to get two children into a routine, but it is possible and you naturally find your way into a routine that suits everyone (although it never feels like you'll ever get there at the beginning). It's not as rigid as it was with just one, but it doesn't have to be – I've realized that babies are more adaptable than I thought.'

In the early days your baby won't yet have a routine and will be quite flexible, but your toddler probably does have one, and it will make things much easier for your child if you try and stick to it. Routines give children security and security makes a child happier and more relaxed. I know just how hard it is to be consistent when life around you seems wildly chaotic, but I found trying to keep to my son's normal daily routine helped make my own day less chaotic and easier to manage too. Just don't worry too much if you don't always get there.

• *What to aim for*

Meals, nap times and bedtimes should be at the same time your child is used to – though it doesn't matter who provides the meals or puts your child to bed for their afternoon and evening sleep. Your child will probably need to follow the same bedtime routine that they are used to in order to get to sleep, i.e. bath, story, bed, but again, it doesn't have to be you who does this, and it doesn't matter if some of the extra bits are missed out (all the songs and funny games the two of you concocted) so long as the basics are stuck to. Try and get your child up at the same time each morning too, even if you have to wake them up. Although it might be tempting to let them sleep in and have time for yourself, your child will develop better sleep habits if they have a consistent routine.

Try and make sure your child is able to do all the activities they did before – going to the toddler group or nursery, playing with friends, going to music class, etc. If most of their world stays the same, it will make it easier for them to adjust to the inevitable changes.

• *When things are different*

Not everything can stay the same, of course. There will be times when you can't do the things you would normally do with your elder child because it doesn't fit in with your baby's routine. Don't feel guilty about this. Accepting that sometimes you won't be able to do everything is important, and if one music class or swimming lesson gets missed it's not the end of the world. But if at all possible, don't blame the missed activity on the baby. As Chloe explains: 'I really try not to use (too much) the baby's needs as an excuse to leave the playground, i.e. "We have to go home because Elise is hungry", as I don't want Oliver to blame her for ruining his fun.'

Survival tips for looking after your elder child

Accept that your toddler will be unsettled: be prepared for your toddler to be unsettled in the early days and to give them lots of reassurance – see chapter 6 for more information about typical toddler behaviour.

Compliment your elder child: when people exclaim over your new baby, be ready with a matching compliment for your toddler, e.g. 'Yes, my baby is gorgeous, just like her big brother/sister.'

Have some special time with your toddler: it can be helpful to have a particular time each day that you set aside to be with your elder child. It is otherwise so easy to promise to play that game 'in just a minute' and then find that the minutes have turned into hours, and it's time for bed. The negative effect this has on your child can be easily imagined.

Avoid saying you are busy because of the baby: instead of blaming the baby for things you can't do with your toddler find another reason, such as your hands are full at the moment, but tell them that you'll go later or when you've finished what you're doing.

Looking after yourself

You are spending so much time caring for your two children that you may not have considered for a moment how you are feeling either physically or mentally. But it's important that you do. You need to look after yourself, partly because you will feel better and you are important too, and partly because you will find it much easier to care for your children if you care for yourself.

How you'll feel physically

You may well find that it takes your body slightly longer to recover after the birth this time. Even a quick and easy birth still takes it out of you. All those muscles that have been stretched and pulled for a second time don't spring back quite as quickly as they did, skin seems slacker and everything just takes longer to get back to its pre-pregnancy form.

You will also feel more tired. A statement of the obvious, but it's important not to try and be Superwoman straight away. You've just had a baby, you've got a small child to look after too and if you are breastfeeding your body is busy burning up energy to produce milk.

How you'll feel emotionally

Having a baby is an intensely emotional experience, both for you and for your partner. Being able to talk to each other about how you feel will make things easier – about the overwhelming love you feel, as well as the magnitude of the responsibilities you face. But mothers also have the hormonal changes that take place after the birth of a baby to deal with, and this may make you feel extra emotional.

● *Baby blues*

Whether or not you experienced these the first time you may get hit by them this time. Up to around 70 per cent of women get the baby blues – that short phase when you become extra emotional and sensitive, suddenly bursting into tears, and swinging from feeling depressed and lethargic and headachy one minute to being ecstatic and hyperactive the next. It usually occurs three or four days after your baby is born and lasts not more than a week. Remember it is temporary, and usually by the second week you begin to feel better physically and emotionally.

● *When it's more serious – postnatal depression*

Approximately 10 per cent of mothers will develop postnatal depression (PND), which can be a serious medical condition and require medical help. It can start within a month of giving birth or not until six months later and it can last for weeks or several months. There is a slightly higher risk of developing it after a second baby because stress and exhaustion – both factors in causing it – are that much higher. Difficulties in your pregnancy and birth may make it more likely, as may having a baby that is difficult to look after or previous experiences of depression or a change in circumstances, but not necessarily. You may not have ever suffered from any sort of depression before, your marriage may be fine and everything up until this point quite happy, but it can still hit you. Health visitors are trained to look out for it and may ask you to fill out a questionnaire called the Edinburgh Postnatal Depression score about how you're feeling. They are looking for symptoms similar to the baby blues but much worse and including:

* feelings of hopelessness
* an inability to care for yourself or your family
* negative feelings towards your baby
* loss of appetite

* loss of energy
* feelings of despair.

Because many women are so ashamed to have these feelings, believing that somehow it is their fault, and that they are failing as a mother, they are reluctant to tell anyone about it. Family health adviser Ruth Fromow has seen this happen: 'People don't tell the truth. I think they worry that if they admit to being depressed then the health visitors will come round more often, which they don't want. I wish people would be honest, even if they don't say anything to the health visitor. Talk to somebody. If you don't tell anyone, you can't get help.'

If you can, talk to your partner about how you are feeling, or family and friends. You don't need to go through this alone and it will be much easier if you don't try to. Don't feel guilty, it isn't your fault. Support from them and getting enough rest may be all that is needed to start feeling better, but not always. Medication may be necessary for things to improve, though it can still take several months, but you will feel better and your life will start to become more manageable again.

● *Postnatal psychosis*

This is the most severe form of postnatal depression and is, luckily, extremely rare. It may include symptoms such as hallucinations, confusion, paranoia, strange behaviour and sleep problems. If you are experiencing any of these, then it is extremely important to speak to a doctor or midwife to get immediate medical help.

Get help

Almost everything will be easier if you can get some sort of help. If you didn't get any help after your first child was born you may think you don't need it this time either. You may think that as you'll have to manage on your own some day you might as well start from the very beginning and that it's just as hard work having to tell someone else what to do as it is to do it yourself, but for the first few days and weeks it really can make an enormous difference to have people who can help out. In these first few weeks you need to have the time just to concentrate on your new family without having to worry about vacuuming the sitting room or cleaning the bathroom. It doesn't mean you're not managing if you accept help, whether from friends and family, or more professional help.

● *Your friends and family*

If you are lucky you will have family close by with whom you feel comfortable and who can offer real support without being asked. But sometimes even the best of friends and family need a bit of direction to know what would be the most helpful thing for them to do. Don't

Ideas for how people can help

* Sit with your baby for an hour so you can read or play a game with your first child.
* Play a game or read a book with your first child so you can spend a quiet time feeding your baby.
* Sit with both your children so you can get a bit of sleep.
* Spend an hour tackling the mountain of ironing.
* Bring over a meal for you to eat with your children.
* Pop to the shops to buy whatever you forgot to order online.
* Put away the shopping that's still in bags in the kitchen.
* Get a DVD for you to watch with your first child.

be shy. These are the friends and family who really want to help you because they care for you and want to make life easier for you, so let them, say thank you and breathe a huge sigh of relief.

Perhaps the best help that your friends can give is just to be there for you to talk to, either on the other end of the telephone or to pop in for a cup of coffee and a chat. Friends who've already had two children and know exactly what you're going through are invaluable. They can offer not just practical help but also advice based on their own experience as well as their knowledge of you and your elder child. A friend who is happy to listen to you, be sympathetic, swap stories of their difficulties with two, tell you that you're doing brilliantly just to have fed, cleaned and dressed both children even if you're still in your pyjamas at midday, and make you laugh, can be the most effective therapy you need.

> **Tip:** If you know you will find it more stressful than helpful to have your mother or mother-in-law to stay, find a polite way of putting her off. Suggest she comes a bit later when your partner has gone back to work, or when you feel more settled.

● *Paid help*

If you don't have any family close by and the thought of having your in-laws to stay for a week fills you with dread, or if you still find it difficult to ask friends to help with more menial tasks, then you might want to consider paying someone to help you. Even if housework has never been your number one priority and you've taken to heart all the good advice about letting the housework go for a few weeks after the baby is born, it can be demoralizing to see just how quickly your house descends into chaos. Paying someone to come and clean for a few hours a week, or to do the ironing, or tidy up the kitchen, or clean the sheets can give you a lift you didn't even know you needed.

● *Hire a maternity nurse or doula*

If you can afford it and have the space, you could consider hiring a maternity nurse who will come to live with you for anything up to a month after your baby is born, getting up in the night to bring you your baby and doing other baby-care related duties night and day. Helping your baby establish a night-time feeding routine so you have more energy to cope in the day is one of the greatest services they can offer a new mother of two. But a cheaper option is a doula. You may not even have heard of a doula (pronounced 'doola'), but an increasing number of women in the UK have and are turning to them for help after their baby is born. A postnatal doula is a specially trained woman who cares for mother and baby during the first couple of weeks after delivery. The word comes from the Greek meaning 'woman servant or caregiver' and if the concept makes you feel slightly uncomfortable, you should under-stand that the service they provide is designed to do the exact opposite. They can work flexible hours to suit you and will help with practical and emotional support in the crucial post-delivery weeks. Tania, who hired a doula for three weeks after her second son, Xan, was born found the help she got a lifesaver: 'My eldest had just gone to school, half days only, so needed quite a bit of attention and I had full-blown flu twice in the first month, so I couldn't have done it without a doula. She did school runs, made lunches, and looked after me while I looked after the baby. With her help I could spend time with both my children.'

● *Share the responsibility with your partner*

Unless you are a single mum, having two children is not just your responsibility, but one that you share with your partner. Provided your partner has been in his job with the same company for long enough (twenty-six weeks by the fourteenth week before your baby was due), he is entitled to two weeks' paternity leave. This doesn't have to be taken all in one go, but with your second child you may be very grateful if your partner can be around to help for this length of time, if not longer. One father admitted to feeling a bit of a spare part after their first child was born: 'I wasn't really sure what I could do that was at all useful. Lezanne was breastfeeding so obviously I couldn't help with that, and there didn't seem much point in getting up in the night just to keep her company. In fact having always been a light sleeper before, I learned to sleep much more deeply after Dillon was born so I didn't get woken up. Mostly I did errands like the shopping. I did the washing and cooked a few suppers but apart from that there wasn't much involvement with looking after the baby. Lezanne's mum lived close by so she was there to help with that and Dillon was an easy baby so he was either feeding or sleeping. In the end I figured the most useful thing I could do was to earn some more money so I went back to work a few days early.'

With a second baby, working out ways in which your partner can help should be easier. For a start, you both have a better idea of what's involved in looking after a newborn baby and what's needed. You will probably remember what happened with your first baby and the demands that were made on you and how you both coped. Some experts recommend actually writing down what helped, and how you felt about the level of help you gave each other. This way you can help avoid any resentment that can so easily build up about who is doing the most work. Some fathers may be longing to help but need their partner to tell them what to do, so again writing a list can be useful. Being organized is an essential part of coping with two children!

Work out together what needs doing, which areas you need help with and how the help can be given:

* If the mum gets up in the night to feed the baby, who gets up if your first child wakes in the night?
* Who will get the first child up, dressed and breakfasted?
* Who will cook the meals?
* Do the housework?
* What about bath-time?
* And bedtime?

For many families, the obvious way to split the duties is for Mum to look after the baby and Dad to look after your first child. The bond between your first child and their dad often becomes very strong in the first weeks after the new baby is born, and this can be wonderful. It can also be hard for you, however appreciative you are of the time it gives you to be with the new baby. You may miss not being able to do the things you always did together, miss the closeness and find it hard when they ask for 'Daddy to do it', and apparently not want or need you any more. If this is the case, just remind yourself that you will soon have more time to spend with your older child, and that your newborn baby will shortly settle into some sort of routine. Try not to interfere too much in your partner's parenting skills with your firstborn, unless you think your child is finding things very confusing. Just because you always sing the toothbrush song after bath-time doesn't mean that's the way it has to be done.

But it's important not to let the division of labour become too segregated. Your partner needs to be able to do some things with the new baby so he can get to know your baby too and have time to bond. Helping with feeding may be out if you are breastfeeding, but he can do all the other things and, like you, will feel more confident handling a baby this time. This gives you the opportunity to spend some special time with your elder child, as well as to get a bit of rest too. Take it in turns to spend some time with each child. And of course doing things all together as a family, like a walk in the park, or just watching a film together can be best of all – what being a family is really all about.

Having two children is not just about the work that is involved but also about the enjoyment that can be shared.

Survival tips for looking after yourself

Do your pelvic floor exercises: you may remember being advised to do these after your first child to strengthen the pelvic floor muscles. These are the exercises where you have to imagine trying to stop yourself weeing or pooing and which you can do anywhere, any time, if you remember. Which you usually don't, or at least not much, and it doesn't really seem to matter. Second time around, all I can say is *do them*! Not being able to jump on the trampoline may not be particularly important to you but not being able to sneeze or cough without being aware of an embarrassing trickle running down your leg is more inconvenient to say the least. Incontinence affects up to 35 per cent of women after a second childbirth and even more – up to 40 per cent – after a third child. Doing your pelvic floor exercises every day can and hopefully will prevent this from being a problem for you.

Eat healthily: you need to keep up your energy and strength to be able to cope with looking after two children and to be able to breast-feed successfully. This is not the time to diet, no matter how much you want to quickly lose that pregnancy weight, which can be even worse after a second child.

Laugh: people often tell you how important it is to have a sense of humour when looking after children. Ha, ha, ha! As my sister Jen said, 'I used to have a sense of humour, but after two children I think it disappeared for a while.' You can't just make yourself find it amusing when your baby is crying, your toddler is having a tantrum and you've had no sleep. But after these stressful moments, try and look at the situation and realize that in most cases problems don't need to be taken too seriously. Look for the funny side. Talk to friends who can make you laugh about things. And go out with your partner, or a friend, to see a comedy or a show that will make you laugh. It's true that laughter is a great medicine.

Get enough rest: yes, I know you have a newborn baby and a toddler to run around after but particularly in the first few weeks don't expect too much of yourself – looking after the baby, spending time with your first child, doing all the cooking and cleaning and all the usual house-work things. If your partner is around to help, let him do the running around while you stay in bed with your baby when you can. Make the most of any help you get in the early days.

Never go anywhere empty-handed: whether it's taking laundry with you when you go upstairs, or taking the dirty washing when you go downstairs, toys when you move from the sitting room to the bedroom, or picking up the post from the hall as you go to the kitchen, you will save a huge amount of time and energy if you remember to take something with you wherever you go. Becoming good at multi-tasking is an essential part of survival with two children.

Be kind to yourself: it's so easy to look at everyone else around you and to assume that they have got everything worked out perfectly and that you are the only one who gets frazzled and feel as though you are muddling through. Somehow all the other mothers seem to look smil-ingly serene and confident, to have tidy houses and to be coping effort-lessly and calmly with their two well-behaved, well-adjusted children. Try not to make these comparisons – we all have strengths and weak-nesses and other mothers are probably looking at you with wonder and awe too. You are doing a fantastic job.

FOUR

And so to bed: managing sleep with two

'How's the new baby sleeping?' people ask as they look at the bags under your eyes, and your weary, bleary expression, while noticing that you've done the buttons the wrong way up on your cardigan.

'Oh, brilliantly, thanks,' you reply through gritted teeth, 'couldn't be better.' For there are two important things every mother should know about babies and sleep.

1. Never believe them when other mothers tell you how well their babies are sleeping – it's probably not true, and if it is true it will only make you feel depressed.
2. When anyone asks you how well your baby is sleeping, always say 'brilliantly'. Whether it's true or not, you will feel much better.

The thing is people always do ask you this question about a new baby, whether it's your first or your fourth – and it's probably the biggest single worry that most mothers have about how they'll cope when their second baby arrives. You know that if you're getting enough sleep you can cope with almost anything but if you are trying to survive on a few hours a night then the simplest thing is a struggle – and looking after two children is not simple. In a nutshell, getting enough sleep makes the difference between enjoying life with your two children and just getting through it.

But how do you do this when you've got two children? It's bad enough when you've got just one child waking you up in the middle of the night.

After weeks of surviving on what seemed like only one or two hours' sleep a night after Harry was born I remember thinking that it must be unlawful – the Geneva Convention prohibited sleep deprivation as a form of torture so surely it couldn't be allowed for mothers. But at least with one baby you can easily follow the recommended advice to 'sleep when the baby sleeps'. You can catch up on lost night-time sleep during the day. When you have an energetic toddler or preschooler who is desperate for your attention and no longer takes daytime naps, you may find it difficult to catch up on any sleep. And if your toddler/preschooler starts to have problems sleeping at night too, then life can become very difficult indeed. Making sure both your baby and toddler sleep well so that you can too seems to be the key to staying calm and enjoying life with two children.

Will you ever get enough sleep again?

Getting your two children to sleep and surviving may prove to be easier than you think. When I asked a group of mothers to fill in a questionnaire about how they coped when their second baby arrived, many mothers wrote that while they were very worried about how they'd manage beforehand, their fears of sleep deprivation with two were unfounded.

Mums on early days with their second child:

'I was really worried about the broken nights at the beginning and not being able to get enough sleep to cope in the day – our first child took nine months before he started to sleep through the night. Second time around it was much easier. Fred slept well from the beginning, only waking every four hours for a feed at night, and by this time Oscar was a good sleeper too – sleeping through the night. During the day we all had a nap in the afternoon. I needn't have worried at all.'

Gillian, mother of Oscar and Fred

'We have been blessed with two very good boys and have been lucky sleep wise. They have shared a room since I stopped breastfeeding Albie at ten weeks. Personally, I think it is much easier with the second as you know what you need them to do.'

Nancy, mother of Stan and Albie

'I panicked when I was awake for ages in the night, thinking that I would be so exhausted the following day. But rarely did I feel so tired that I couldn't function properly. When things were bad (in the early days), I used to think any sleep was a bonus (not a given), which made me feel better.'

Chloe, mother of Oliver and Elise

'The two children just slipped into routines easily. As I was bottle feeding it made it easier for my husband to help out, so sleep wasn't really a problem.'

Sue, mother of Alice and Robbie

It's impossible to predict how much sleep you'll get. Newborn babies are meant to sleep an average of sixteen hours a day, but yours may not. Some babies will sleep easily and for several hours at a time, and others need more help to get to sleep and still only stay asleep for short periods. There's the added problem that your sleep might be disturbed by your older child being unsettled by the arrival of their new baby. But on the positive side, there are various factors in your favour that make it likely you will find it easier to get your baby to sleep this time.

You are a more experienced mum so:

* you may find feeding easier, which will help your baby sleep better
* you will have learned some tricks about getting babies to sleep and, as Nancy said, 'know what you need them to do'
* you won't be so anxious to 'check' on your baby
* you know your toddler's personality and sleep habits.

With your experience and confidence and a bit of luck you may find that the broken nights don't last too long, so that soon you are able to tell people truthfully how brilliantly you are all sleeping.

Getting your baby into a routine

Whatever you thought about routines with your first child, for most mothers with a second baby, getting them into some sort of routine is the Holy Grail. I'm not talking about a strict routine where everything has to be done by the clock, and which can make you feel a dreadful failure if you can't achieve it, but a flexible routine that gives you a sense of emerging out of chaos into order.

With their second babies many mothers decide that the way to do this is to start a sleep routine as soon as possible. 'With our first child we spent many weeks trying to get him to sleep in the evenings,' Chloe explained. 'I knew this time that I wanted to crack that straight away (as I really needed to have the evenings to relax), so we started a bedtime routine with Elise pretty early on, which worked well. We got our evenings back very quickly this time around.'

Nancy did the same thing: 'Every night at 7pm from the moment I brought Albie back from hospital I would fill him with milk via a bottle (either expressed or formula) and put him down to sleep in a dark quiet room. We got a bath/bedtime routine going as soon as possible to teach the baby about bedtime.'

Bedtime routine

You will be feeding your baby roughly every three or four hours through the day and night in the first few weeks, but you can start to teach your baby the difference between day and night by putting your baby to bed at bedtime, right from the start.

Follow the same bedtime routine that you do with your toddler – i.e. at the same time each night bath your baby, change them into their night-time sleep clothes, feed them and put them down in their cot and say goodnight. See what happens – they may sleep for a solid four hours. Your baby is too little to start a controlled crying programme (where you leave your baby to cry for increasing lengths of time before going in to reassure them), but as a second-time mother if your baby does cry you are more likely to know whether your baby is crying from hunger, or wants to be held and comforted or whether there's another reason. You will know not to rush in the second you hear a cry but to allow them a minute or two to settle themselves back to sleep.

During the day

You can also start aiming for a routine during the day from the beginning. The key to establishing a successful daytime routine with a second baby is flexibility. You probably can't spend all day indoors putting your second baby down to sleep in their cot every couple of hours. Instead you need to find a routine that fits in with your toddler's activities and your busy schedule – so your baby may have to nap in the buggy in the morning as you take your toddler to toddler group and sleep in the car in the afternoon as you drive to another activity. But try to start and end your baby's daily routine at the same time each day, fitting in three or four daytime naps of about an hour-and-a-half in length somewhere in between. Also, consider the following:

Beware overtired babies: don't keep your baby awake for too long in the hope that they will sleep longer at night-time. Babies get easily overtired if they are awake for longer than a couple of hours at a stretch and find it harder to get to sleep the longer they have been up. Try putting your baby down for a nap in their cot or in a comfortable place to sleep every two hours and see if this does the trick.

Blackout blinds: most experts agree that it is helpful to put your baby to sleep in a darkened room. If your baby is sleeping in your room to begin with (see below), and you don't have wonderfully thick lined curtains, then do invest in blackout blinds. (This is particularly important if you have a summer baby.) It's worth buying them, even if you do only need them for a relatively short period of time.

Noise machine: turning on a low background noise before putting your baby down to sleep is particularly helpful for getting a second baby to sleep. The gentle humming sound drowns out the other noises in the house – your toddler running up and down the stairs, making car noises, etc. – and babies seem to find the repetitive noise soothing.

You can buy special noise machines that produce white noise sounds or relaxing sounds of nature, such as the wind or waves. Alternatively you can buy CDs of these sounds.

Co-ordinating your baby and toddler's bedtime routine

It is bedtime and you want to get both your baby and toddler to sleep with as little fuss as possible and still have some evening left to yourself. How do you do it?

You have two options:

1. Staggering bedtimes – put one child to bed, and then the other.
2. Simultaneous bedtimes – put both children to bed at the same time.

If you don't have any help and you have to manage putting both children to bed on your own, co-ordinating bedtimes is more of a challenge.

● *Staggering bedtimes*

The advantage of this method is that you can concentrate on each child and spend one-to-one time with them. The disadvantage is that you spend much more of your evening putting your children to bed.

It usually works best to do the baby's bedtime first, so that your older child doesn't feel too resentful at being put to bed before the baby and can enjoy the 'privilege' of staying up later. If your older child is happy playing quietly in their bedroom while you put the baby to bed and before it's their turn, that's great. If not, your older child may enjoy helping you to bath the baby and changing them into their sleep clothes and then listening to a story with you while you feed the baby. Knowing that they will have your undivided attention for their bath and bedtime story once the baby is asleep will usually act as a fairly good incentive for them to be quiet while the baby is going off to sleep. This doesn't always work, and you may find that in the first few weeks your baby is particularly awake in the early evening. In this case you will need to do your older child's bedtime routine first while your baby is in their Moses basket and then turn your attention to the baby later.

● *Simultaneous bedtimes*

This is the time-saving option, but it requires excellent multi-tasking skills. In the early days, if you've got help and your partner is around, putting both children to bed at the same time is easy. Your partner can bath your first child while you bath and feed the baby and put them to bed in the cot or crib. If your partner has followed your older child's usual bedtime routine (assuming they have one) – brushed teeth, potty/loo, bedtime story, you can then go in to your child's bedroom to kiss them goodnight before heaving a sigh of relief and going downstairs to relax, until the baby's next feed.

If you haven't got help, trying to get both your baby and toddler bathed, into sleep wear and into bed at the same time is hard work but not impossible.

Here are some tips for successful bath-times.

* First get all towels, nappies, pyjamas and night dresses ready.
* There are a number of ways of bathing your baby and toddler at the same time:
    * You can bath your baby separately in a baby bath in the bathroom while you keep an eye on your toddler in the big bath.

* Some baby baths have an extra wide rim so will fit onto an adult bath and your baby and toddler can bath at the same time (make sure the baby bath will fit the adult bath before you buy it though).

* You can put your baby in a baby bucket bath, which you can put in the big bath. Your baby is kept in an upright position in the bucket bath so you have both hands free to bath them and your toddler at the same time.

* One at a time: bath your baby in the big bath first, rub dry, put on sleep suit and sit in bouncy seat, then add a little more water and bath your toddler.

I waited until Rory was about six months before bathing him in the same bath as Harry, but they soon loved sharing a bath together.

Separate bedtimes

Family health adviser Ruth Fromow advises that for slightly older children separate bedtimes is the best way to avoid resentment between siblings who are sharing a room. Many children who are close in age are made to go to bed at the same time if they share a room because it's thought to be easier, but this can often lead to resentment on the part of the older child who feels that they should not be treated the same as 'the baby'. Even if the older child only keeps their bedside light on for an extra ten minutes, this can be enough to make a difference and for the older child to feel more grown-up. It doesn't have to mean that the older child actually goes to bed later but they get to stay awake for a little longer.

Once your baby and toddler are clean and in their sleep things, it's time for a story, then bed. This is how Sam managed it: 'After bath-time we'd all go to my bedroom and sit in my double bed. The lights would be dimmed and I took the phone off the hook. I'd feed my baby and my toddler would sit next to me so we could read a book. After this, we'd sing a few songs quietly. When I'd finished feeding and winding the baby I'd put her in the cot, still just awake but sleepy and then take my toddler to her bed and say goodnight. That was it. I did the same thing every night and it worked a treat.'

Where should your baby, toddler and you sleep?

For the first six months, your baby should sleep in a cot or crib in your bedroom. That's the recommended advice in the UK from the Foundation for the Study of Infant Deaths (FSID) as being the safest place. Of course, in the early days, your baby will also sleep in all sorts of other places, wherever they feel most comfortable – in a sling as you carry them around, in the car as you drive to the shops, in the buggy as you walk to the park, but for scheduled sleeps, a cot in your bedroom is the best place. It makes sense too as you can easily check that your baby is all right at night and it makes it easier to get to your baby for night-time feeding. Not all dads feel quite the same way and I certainly know of several dads who found it easier to sleep in the spare room for the first few months to get an uninterrupted night's sleep so that they could function properly at work – or even that the mother and baby moved in to the spare room to allow their partner to sleep better in their bedroom!

If your older child has been happily sleeping in their own room, this can continue and the frequent night feedings won't interrupt your child. But some children find it quite hard to understand why the baby is allowed to sleep in your room and they are not. If this is the case, you need to explain that the baby will only be in your room for a short time while they are waking in the night and that soon they will move into a separate room.

From six months your baby can move out of your bedroom and either share a bedroom with your older child or sleep in a separate bedroom. By this time your baby should be working towards sleeping twelve hours a night.

What about co-sleeping?

This is a subject that people feel strongly about one way or another so, with some nervousness, I have to confess that I ended up with all four of my babies in bed with me – though not at the same time, obviously. This was not an intentional plan – I didn't think to myself that I must do it to bond better with my baby, or to give my baby a greater sense of security – I did it mostly because I fell asleep. The babies would be put to sleep in their cot at the beginning of the evening but after one of the middle-of-the-night feeds, they would come into my bed and that is where they'd stay. I'd feed lying down and sort of doze, and the baby would happily feed away for as long as he wanted. It meant I got far more sleep – was less tired in the morning – and did actually feel very bonded to each of my babies. For those of you not horrified, I can recommend it (provided you don't drink or smoke – see the FSID website for information on safe conditions for co-sleeping). However, this period of babies sleeping in my bed lasted only for as long as they were feeding in the middle of the night – after that they stayed in their separate cots. If you have decided to let your first baby continue to sleep in your bed, you may have a problem when your second baby comes along – the general advice is that a baby and a small toddler should not sleep in the same bed for safety reasons. It will be unsettling to say the least if your older child is moved out of your bed so the new baby can replace them. So either consider moving your toddler into a room and bed of their own some time in advance of your new baby's arrival or think of another way of keeping your toddler close by – putting an extra bed or mattress in your bedroom for them to sleep on, for example.

Moving your toddler into a big bed

The arrival of a new baby is often the time parents consider moving their first child into a big bed. If you think your child is ready for it (you go into their room one morning to discover that they have scaled the bars of the cot and are happily teetering on the top) the solution is to move them before the baby is born. Even if the baby will be sleeping in a crib for the first few months and you don't need the cot straight away, it's still better to move your child some time before the baby is born rather than just afterwards. The temptation a child may have to visit you in your room once they discover they can get out of bed whenever they want needs to be sorted out well before you are also trying to keep a baby asleep in your room! Additionally you don't want your child to feel they are being moved out of their cot in order for the baby to sleep in it – moving them into a big bed on one day and the baby into the cot the next will do little to improve feelings of sibling jealousy.

But don't try and move your baby out of their cot if they are not ready. If they are still sleeping happily and securely in their cot, and you think they could do so for quite some months after your baby is born, then it is worth borrowing a crib or cot for your baby to sleep in until your older child really does need to move.

It's a big milestone when your child moves out of their cot – seeing them in a bed makes them seem suddenly so grown-up – and it can be exciting but a bit unsettling for your child too. To make the transition as smooth as possible, get your child involved in deciding what sort of bed linen they'd like and where to put the bed. If your child is allowed a beautiful pink Barbie duvet cover or a Peppa Pig pillow case they'll be longing to go to bed (it's worth it, so you'll just have to swallow your aesthetic principles).

> **Tip:** Keep the bed in the same place as the cot was because it's what your child is used to. A different perspective of the room at night-time might make it harder for your child to go to sleep. If this means that one side of the bed is against the wall you need to make sure that your child cannot get wedged in down the side.

It's worth spending a bit of time on choosing the right sort of bed for your older child too, bearing in mind that one day your baby will also need to move into a bed. The expense of buying a special toddler-sized bed, which will soon be grown out of, may make sense if it can be used for your baby too, but then what about the design? Those novelty beds designed in the shape of cars, castles or fairy bowers may help to make your older child want to go to bed, but will your baby son want to sleep in your daughter's fairy bower when it's his turn to sleep in the bed? My oldest son always longed for one of those high beds with a slide at one end. I'm afraid he never got his heart's desire because I knew he'd be up all night sliding down the slide, keeping his baby brother awake – and the rest of the household too. Instead, we bought a bunk bed because we knew that one day the two children would share a room and that by the time the baby was old enough to sleep in a bed, Harry would be old enough to sleep on the top bunk. Although we didn't have the top bed put up at the beginning (that would have been asking for trouble), we used the top bunk bed as the bottom bed because it had guard rails that stopped Harry from falling out at night (though it didn't stop him from using the bed as a trampoline and bouncing out over the rails).

Where space isn't an issue, many parents, according to recent statistics, are moving their children into full-size or even double beds right from the start. The idea is that a larger-sized bed not only allows for more freedom of movement while your child is asleep, but it also means there's enough room for you to lie on the bed with your child and share bedtime stories together. Instead of your bed becoming the family bed where your children snuggle up for a bedtime story before being carried to their own beds, your child's bed can be where you all pile in – alternating with their sibling's bed every night. Where siblings become very close, they may actually want to share a bed and can do so comfortably if the bed is big enough.

Whatever sort of bed your child ends up being moved into, be prepared to spend a few evenings getting your child to stay in it. It may take several nights of firmly returning your child to bed – without talking to them and giving them extra attention – before they realize that there is nothing to be gained by getting out of bed, so they might as well stay there. Even then, it's hard to stop a small child from getting out of their bed and climbing into yours while you're fast asleep in the middle of the night.

Should your baby and toddler share a room?

So long as you have made sure that the bedroom is safe for the two of them – that your older child can't get to toys, which, if passed through the bars of the baby's cot could be dangerous, and that any tall furniture is fixed securely and can't accidentally be pushed by a toddler over onto the cot – then there's no reason why not. In the not so old days, it was usual for the baby to be put in their older sibling's room once they were sleeping through the night. Siblings would not only share a room but sometimes a bed too. In fact quite often whole families shared a room – like Charlie in Roald Dahl's *Charlie and the Chocolate Factory* where the four grandparents sleep in one bed in the same room as Charlie and his mum and dad. But even if, unlike Charlie, you do have the space and spare bedrooms, many parents find that their young children get extra comfort and security from sharing a bedroom. As their children get a little bit older, parents believe that it encourages siblings to be closer; that they are bound to share whispered secrets and stories after lights out, and enjoy the obligatory pillow fights; that sleeping in the same room teaches children how to have respect for each other and be more tolerant towards each other. A few months after the arrival of the new baby, many parents put their children in the same room, because they believe it will foster a loving and giving relationship.

That's one theory. The other theory is that children need to have their own private space, where they can do what they like and express their individuality, a bedroom to call their own. If you try and make children share a room, you'll only be creating massive problems. A child who suddenly has to share their bedroom with a new baby may feel angry and resentful. Instead of making children bond together and feel closer, sharing a room makes brothers and sisters more likely to fight, and be angry with each other. The stress that it may cause in an older child when the new baby is put into their bedroom, which they've been used to having all to themselves, may lead to sleep problems such as frequent night awakenings or wetting the bed. On top of that there are the problems of the children waking each other up in the night or too early in the morning. As they get older and their personalities and their own individual tastes develop, the problems are likely to get worse. They can't escape from each other – they can't even have friends round for a sleepover.

My personal view is that it entirely depends on the temperament and personalities of your children. I was made to share with my sister – and we definitely got on better when we later had separate bedrooms. My boys shared a room when they were little and this created a closeness that was later lost when they had bedrooms of their own. As children get older, the need for their own independent space often becomes greater and it's important to listen to them and check how they are feeling about sharing.

● *Helping your baby and toddler enjoy sharing a room*
Whether or not to put your two children into the same room may all be academic if you don't have an extra bedroom. Your children may just have to share a bedroom. Here are some ideas and tips to minimize the possibility of problems and so that your first child does not mind the new baby moving into their bedroom:

* Try to organize the bedroom so that both your baby and toddler can have their own separate space within it. A room that allows the children to be together when they want to be but also to be private in their own sanctuary is ideal and it doesn't necessarily require a lot of space to achieve.

* Involve your child as much as possible. Ask them where they would like to have their bed and where they think the baby's cot should go.
* Use furniture such as bookshelves, desks or a wardrobe to divide the bedroom into two separate areas.
* Divide the room by painting it two different colours.
* Have things at different heights for your older child and the baby. Low bookshelves, toy boxes and coat pegs for the baby; higher ones for your older child.
* If the children are sharing a wardrobe, have two separate rails – a low one and a higher one. Make two distinct areas of the wardrobe for the baby and child with different types of lining paper.
* Cupboards and drawers can be identified by painting them different colours for each child.
* Keep the room tidy: teach your children from as early as possible how to keep their bedroom tidy. Toddlers know where their toys and clothes go and can easily learn how to put things away – especially if you make a game out of it. By helping your children keep their bedroom organized and not a chaotic muddle where neither child can find their own things and start to look in the other child's territory, you reduce a potential area of conflict. There is a famous family story when my sister and I shared a room and I, unable to find any pants, decided to look for them in my sister's drawer on her side of the wardrobe. This provoked outraged fury and a hairbrush being thrown – with great accuracy – and breaking my tooth. Such small things can engender such big passions! Teaching your children to respect each other's possessions is vital for their safety and your sanity.

● *Will your baby and toddler wake each other up?*

It's the scenario every mother dreads. You've just got both children to sleep after an hour of patiently reading stories, kissing bears and singing songs. You oh-so-quietly tiptoe out of the bedroom, flinching when that loose floorboard you promised yourself you'd nail down creaks, you make it down the stairs and to the fridge to open that bottle of wine or pick up the telephone to make that call to your sister when you hear it. 'Waaaaggh' – you race back upstairs to try and pick up the baby before they wake your child. Too late! Your toddler has woken up too, and now you've got to get them both back to sleep all over again.

This may happen a few times, but it's amazing how much noise children can sleep through without being woken up, especially once they are in deep sleep. This occurs in babies and young children within about twenty minutes of going to sleep, and after that time you can have a party and turn the volume up loud without worrying, so your baby and toddler are very unlikely to wake each other up. Ruth Fromow, family health adviser, agrees: 'Mostly babies don't wake up the toddler. The thing is not to rush in to pick up the baby the minute they cry for fear of waking up the toddler. If you give the baby a few minutes before you go in, the chances are that the baby will settle itself back to sleep without waking their older sibling at all.'

Miranda found that putting her children to bed in the same room helped them to get to sleep without her: 'We put our five-month-old baby in the same bedroom with his nearly three-year-old big brother and it's been a great success. They are both sleepy but awake when we say goodnight and turn the light out. I close the door and you can hear them chatting away to each other for a while and then they just both fall asleep. Before then I used to spend ages with Jack before he'd go to sleep.'

Children are immensely adaptable and your older child will quickly learn not to let the baby's snuffles, breathing and other sounds disturb them. Sometimes the sound of the sleeping child's regular breathing can actually help the child who is awake to settle to sleep. If both your baby and toddler have learned how to settle themselves back to sleep without needing an adult to help them back to sleep, even light awakenings won't trouble them.

● *What to do when they do disturb each other*
Having said that, if either your toddler or your baby – or both – has problems going to sleep or staying asleep, and regularly wakes up in the night disturbing the other one, it is better to keep the children separate until you have resolved the problem. There are many books and websites offering advice for solving sleep problems. They usually involve an element of leaving the baby/toddler to cry for increasingly longer periods of time until the child learns how to go back to sleep on their own. While this is happening, the 'good sleeper' should be allowed to sleep in a different room – even if it has to be your bedroom.

As your baby and toddler get older you may find that the problem is not that they wake each other up at night but that they keep each other from going to sleep in the first place. When this happens the best thing is to separate them. Give them a warning first, but if they carry on as if they'd never heard you, then you'll have to move one child into another room for the night.

Sleep problems that emerge in your toddler when the new baby comes home

Your older child may have been a great sleeper and then the new baby arrives and suddenly they start to have sleep problems. They may start waking up several times in the night and calling for you, they may start waking up too early in the morning or they may start to wet the bed again, having been dry for months. Stressful as this is for you, trying to manage on little enough sleep as it is, your child's sleep problems are probably an indication that they are stressed too. A sensitive child can find the arrival of a new baby very stressful and they need extra patient loving care and attention.

The good news is that sleep problems caused by the arrival of a new baby usually sort themselves out within a few months. Continuing with a consistent and calm bedtime routine helps, as does talking to your child and listening to them if they are old enough to be able to express how they are feeling and to tell you what is worrying them. If your child is constantly waking in the night, you will need to be reassuring but firm and put them back in their own bed. However tempting it might be to bring them into your bed, this may encourage your child to continue waking at night just so that they can share your bed.

Tip: Star charts can work well for a variety of sleep problems. Giving your child a star for every night they stay in bed or don't wet the bed, with a reward at the end of a whole week of stars, can act as a powerful motivator!

Daytime naps

'If you do nothing else ... just try and make sure you get both kids to have a nap at the same time every day – this was my sanity' – Nancy, mother of Stan and Albie.

You may think it's impossible to sleep during the day now that you have two children, and that the days of 'sleeping while your child sleeps' are long gone – especially if your older child has decided that they no longer need or want a nap during the day. But this doesn't have to be the case, and for many mothers the afternoon nap is what keeps them going.

Most toddlers up until the age of three need twelve to thirteen hours' sleep a day including a nap. If you're worried that your older child won't sleep so well at night if they sleep during the day, don't be. Research shows that children who have a nap at the right time of day and for the right length of time actually sleep better at night than children who don't. So even if your older child is determined that they don't want a sleep during the day, it's worth doing what you can to encourage them.

How to get everyone to take a nap

Treat nap-time a bit like bedtime and have a consistent routine that you use each day. Just after lunch when everyone – adults and children – has a normal dip in energy is the best time to try:

* Spend as much time as you can in the morning doing things with your toddler to use up their energy. Going for a walk to the park or going to a baby and toddler group will help your child to feel tired.

* Many children start refusing naps when the baby sleeps because they want to spend this time with you. So when your baby is asleep in the morning, spend this time doing something with your older child so that they have had some of your undivided attention. If you've already spent some one-to-one time with them they may be more willing – and tired enough – to take an afternoon nap.

* Although a toddler won't readily admit to being tired, the signs may well be there that they are. Watch out for your child becoming quieter or alternatively more fussy and whiny and prone to tantrums, or they start rubbing their eyes and yawning.

Many mothers, like Foo, found the best way of getting her baby and toddler to sleep in the afternoon was to all get into the double bed together. She read stories to three-year-old Oscar while she was feeding Hugo. Hugo, full of milk and sleepy, would then be put down in the cot while she and Oscar shared a few more stories before going to sleep together for an hour in the big bed.

The advantage of sleeping while your children sleep is that you catch up on some much needed rest. The disadvantage for some mothers is that you lose that precious time for yourself.

Quiet time

If you don't manage to get your older child to actually go to sleep when your baby naps in the afternoon, it is worth aiming for a period of quiet time instead. During this time, while you put your baby down for their sleep, tell your first child that they must do something quietly for, say, half-an-hour in their bedroom – looking at books, drawing, listening to story tapes. You could have special toys and books that are kept just for playing with at this time of day and which don't need you to help them with. Alternatively you could let them watch a DVD. The idea is that this is something they do on their own so that everyone has time to recharge their batteries. It also encourages your child to learn how to play by themselves without always being entertained. After half-an-hour – or however long you think you can reasonably expect your child to be quiet for – go into your child's room and spend the rest of the time while your baby is asleep playing with them. That's their reward for playing quietly. You may find it helps your child, and you, to have a timer so that they know when quiet time is over and shared one-to-one time can start.

Survival tips for getting enough sleep and coping with tiredness

Sleep when you can: 'Take any opportunity to sleep. If someone offers to take your baby for a walk, put your toddler to bed and go to bed and take a nap yourself. Seek out helpful teenagers who love playing with babies, or toddlers, or even better, both, so you can get some rest and time to yourself.' Gayle, mother of Theo, Katia and Adelaide.

Watch what you eat and drink: 'Very strong coffee was the only thing that would wake me up in the morning and keep me going, although I couldn't do this when I was breastfeeding. Also I had to limit my caffeine drinks to before lunchtime otherwise I found I couldn't get to sleep in the evening, no matter how tired I was.' Liz, mother of Joseph and Miles.

Boosting energy: 'I used to keep a bunch of bananas by my bed, and a jug of water. While I was feeding in the middle of the night I'd eat a banana and drink my water and this gave me the energy I really needed then.' Gina, mother of Daniel and Finn.

Plan ahead when driving: one of the most frightening times for me was when I was driving on the motorway with my two children in the car and feeling so tired that I thought I might fall asleep at the wheel. Pinching myself, opening the windows, turning the radio up didn't work, though fear got the adrenaline going until I could stop at the next service station. I couldn't take a nap, but I got both children out and walked around. The fresh air and exercise revived me so I was able to finish the journey. But I would strongly recommend postponing a long drive by car with your children if you've had very little sleep the night before, or otherwise get someone to share the driving with.

Morning sleep: 'I was lucky that my husband worked from home so at 6am-ish, he was able to take both the children for a couple of hours (and do breakfast) and I could have a really deep sleep, which made a massive difference.' Chloe, mother of Oliver and Elise.

Express and sleep: 'Expressing milk was what got me through the first few months. It meant I could go to bed as early as 8pm if I wanted and my husband could do the first night-time feed. I'd have uninterrupted sleep until the 2am slot when I'd feed again, but after six hours of sleep that was fine.' Liz, mother of Will and Lucy.

Take it in turns to do night-time feeds: 'I bottle fed, so we took it in turns to be on night duty and did alternate nights.' Nicky, mother of Daniel and Joe.

Weekend lie-ins: 'At weekends, we'd take it in turns to have a lie-in in the morning. This meant that on Saturday, which was my turn to lie in, my husband would get up and do both children and I could stay in bed and sleep for as long as I liked. It made the rest of the week bearable, knowing that I'd have that to look forward to.' Anya, mother of Lily and Sophie.

Early to bed: 'At least three times a week I go to bed when the children do. Even if I've got loads of stuff I ought to do, I know I'll get it done better and quicker if I've had enough sleep and am not tired. It's not going to last for ever, this period, so I'm sure I'll have more energy and be less tired soon.' Rachel, mother of Clare and Ben.

Feeding the family: your baby and toddler and you

Can feeding your baby be that different the second time around? Well, yes, actually it can – and third and fourth time round too! For me, breastfeeding Rory, my second baby, was much easier. I knew how to get him to latch on and how to break the latch when it wasn't quite working. I knew how to encourage him to take a full feed, rather than letting him fall asleep after five minutes only to be hungry again ten minutes later. We got into a regular feeding pattern much more quickly this time. I also had more confidence in my choice and worried less about whether he was getting enough. But there were some things that were more difficult. I might have got better and quicker at breast-feeding but it still took up a lot of time each day and keeping Harry, my active, easily bored toddler entertained while I did this was a constant challenge. Learning how to manage the feeding sessions with your baby while looking after your firstborn is one of the biggest differences of breastfeeding second time around.

Most mothers tend to choose the same method of feeding their second child as their first but not all. Perhaps you didn't breastfeed your first child because your child was ill or because you found you were unable to do it but would like to try with your second – or perhaps you feel with a second baby it will be easier to bottle feed this time. There are many ways in which feeding your second baby may be very different from feeding your first.

Breastfeeding

'Breast is best' is the message that the midwives and health visitors have successfully been promoting over recent years and there can't be many women who aren't aware of the various advantages of breast-feeding, even for a short time, both for your baby and for you. For your baby, it's the unique composition of your milk, which adapts to their growing needs and development, strengthening their immune system as well as protecting them against allergies. For you, it's the convenience of breastfeeding, the fact that it's free food, that it makes you sit down and rest (particularly important when you're running around after your toddler most of the day), not to mention all the extra energy you burn up and weight you lose doing it, which are among the most powerful benefits.

Breastfeeding for the first time

There are many reasons why you might not have breastfed your first baby but decide to do so with your second. Perhaps you decided to bottle feed because you had to return to work soon after your first baby was born, but have longer at home with this baby. Or perhaps the other advantages of bottle feeding, such as not needing to worry about what you eat and getting your figure back more quickly, may have seemed more important to you with your first baby than they do now. Perhaps you were ill and on medication with your first baby, but are not now, or perhaps your baby was born with a condition that made it difficult for them to breastfeed.

But for many women, the reason why they didn't breastfeed their first baby was because they tried and found it too hard. I have spoken to mothers who have related shockingly painful stories of putting up with weeks of cracked nipples, blisters, bleeding, blocked milk ducts and the feverish temperatures that go with mastitis, before finally giving up in a state of agony and exhaustion. Other mothers I have spoken to stopped breastfeeding because their babies either couldn't or wouldn't suck properly and 'failed to thrive', that dreadfully clinical term used by the medical profession to describe a baby who isn't getting any bigger and growing as they should. When your baby is crying from hunger, and not putting on weight, the natural thing to do is to go straight to the shop and buy that tin of formula. As one mother said to me, 'I felt such a failure not being able to breastfeed my first child. I had read so much about the bonding experience of breastfeeding but how can you bond with your baby if you're screwing up your eyes in pain and your baby is upset and hungry because you can't do it properly? I felt I couldn't carry on and once I started bottle feeding we were both much happier. But I also knew that I wanted to try breastfeeding again with my second baby and get it right this time.'

So will breastfeeding be easier this time?

The answer is, quite possibly yes. It depends on the reason you found it difficult in the first place:

Not producing enough milk: if this was the reason you were unable to breastfeed your first baby, medical research suggests that you will probably find it easier with a second baby, as women are more likely to produce enough milk second time around.

Pain while feeding: if the reason was because it was so painful – you had mastitis or an abscess, again there is no reason why this should happen a second time. If it does, make sure you get support and advice from your health visitor or GP to see you through this time. It may be that the reason you are experiencing pain while breastfeeding is because you are not getting your baby to latch on properly – your health visitor, or a breastfeeding consultant (see below), can show you how to do this.

Baby didn't take to breastfeeding: anecdotally, several mothers who had problems feeding their first baby told me that they found breastfeeding their second baby much easier, because their baby found it easier. As Anna remembers, 'I found breastfeeding my first child really hard. I had had a Caesarean and everything was painful. Finn didn't suck properly and seemed to lose interest in trying. I gave up and bottle fed, which he found much easier. I knew I wanted to breastfeed my second baby but I was dreading it too. Luckily it was completely different. From the first moment my daughter was put to my breast she seemed to know what to do and everything just worked. No infections, no soreness, it was bliss and I carried on breastfeeding until Emily was nine months old.'

But breastfeeding is not simple, however natural it might be. It takes time and patience to get right. With a young child to look after at the same time you may find learning to do it is even harder. If at all possible, get someone to help you look after your toddler while you spend time with your baby getting breastfeeding established. The more relaxed and the less tired you are, the more likely you are to be successful.

Getting the right support

One of the keys to feeding more successfully second time around is getting the right support and having the confidence to ask for it. Some mothers gave up breastfeeding their first baby because they were not given consistent support or information. Quite a few women told me how they received conflicting advice on how to breastfeed from different people – either from relations, friends or professionals – each with their own methods, with the result that they felt so confused and unhappy they just gave up. Others, like Jane, simply felt unable to ask for help: 'With my first baby, I had problems with him latching on and positioning but my health visitor didn't really look or show me what to do, and because I thought I ought to know what to do if I was a real mother, I didn't properly ask her to show me. When she could see I was struggling, she suggested I try a night-time bottle and I did, and then my milk just seemed to dry up. I knew with my second baby that I really needed more help. I talked to the midwife about it and felt more confident about asking. I think being more experienced and knowing how to get help made a big difference.'

With a second baby many mothers find it easier to be more assertive and know when to ask for help. So do bang on doors until you get it. Whether it's from the health visitor, or an organization like the NCT and La Leche League, or simply advice and support from your network of friends, make sure you get the help you need to make breastfeeding successful with your second baby.

Breastfeeding for the second time

If you enjoyed breastfeeding your first child and were able to do so successfully, you will probably want to do the same thing again with your second. And if so you'll be glad to know that it isn't just mothers who had problems with their first baby who found feeding easier with their second. Many mothers who had found it quite easy with their first baby found it even easier with their second baby. According to Jess, mother of Isobel and Louise, 'Breastfeeding was much easier with my second baby. It hurt much less and my nipples were less sore. This time I knew when to remove my baby if the latch wasn't right.'

Being experienced and knowing what to do makes things easier in other ways as well. Sarah, mother of Issy and Madeleine, says: 'Breastfeeding was an absolute joy with my second. With my first, it took quite a long time to get feeding properly established. I knew what I was doing second time round, so we got into a good feeding schedule early on. I knew how to make sure my baby had fed enough at each feed and I also knew not to feed her instantly every time she cried like I did with my first. If she'd only had a feed quite recently I knew she probably wasn't really hungry and could string her along for a bit until she was hungry enough to feed properly. This meant she slept better too so it really was a lot easier.'

It's a scientific fact too. According to various studies, mothers breastfeeding their second babies are able to do so more quickly, spending about an hour less a day feeding. Being more confident and relaxed with your second baby helps to make breastfeeding both easier and quicker.

What is different?

After-pains: 'Why doesn't anyone tell you about that with your second baby?' a friend said to me the other day. These are the pains you get from your uterus contracting every time you feed, which you probably didn't experience when feeding your first baby (the oxytocin has to work harder to contract your uterus this time), and they can be incredibly painful. More so if you're not expecting them. 'The first four to five days were awful – much worse than with my first baby. Much worse than the sore nipples I got from feeding,' remembers Anna. Maybe the reason no one tells you about them is because they do only last a few days so perhaps memory fades – though I can still remember them quite clearly! There's nothing you can do about them except to take strong painkillers, and to keep telling yourself that they won't last for long.

Your baby: it's also important to point out that the experience of breastfeeding isn't just dependent on how experienced you are as a mother. Babies are different. Some will feed easily right from the start, while others may need a lot of encouragement, feeding only for a short amount of time before dropping off. Some babies may have reflux and not be able to keep their feed down or develop a milk allergy, or something different, and it doesn't matter whether this is your first baby, or your tenth. My fourth son had tongue-tie – something none of my other babies had suffered from – and didn't feed properly for ages. He wasn't putting on weight and I had no idea why. I thought by now I should certainly know how to breastfeed yet here I was with a baby who was failing to thrive. A quick trip to the hospital to have the tie cut and everything was fine again, but it demonstrated to me that there can always be problems, no matter how many babies you've fed before. Nor can you guarantee that you won't have any of the other breastfeeding problems or infections. But on the whole, you are more likely to be more successful breastfeeding your second baby, so if you want to, it's definitely worth giving it a try.

Your first child: as with everything to do with having a second baby, the fact that you have an older child to look after will make a big difference. You will be more tired, have less time, and instead of having one baby to think about, you now have to manage two feeding routines.

Breastfeeding two

If you get pregnant again quickly after your first baby, you might still be breastfeeding (it's not always true that breastfeeding stops you from getting pregnant) and there is no medical reason why you can't carry on breastfeeding your older child right through your pregnancy. It may of course be tiring and you could also find that it becomes more uncomfortable, not just because of your growing bump but also because hormonal changes can cause nipple soreness in pregnancy, which is not helped by feeding. In the later stages of pregnancy, your milk changes to colostrum which your older baby may not like the taste of so much and might decide to stop and become fully weaned. Also you are likely to produce less milk in the later stages of pregnancy, so if your first baby is under six months old you need to just check that they are putting on enough weight.

Because your body releases oxytocin when you breastfeed and this is the same hormone you produce when you go into labour, there have been worries that breastfeeding could start labour. This is not now thought to be the case as your womb doesn't react to oxytocin until after thirty-seven weeks, but if your first baby was premature, or you have had some bleeding before, you might be advised to wean your first baby if you become pregnant again. Talk to your doctor if you're concerned.

If both you and your first baby don't want to stop you can continue to breastfeed your older baby even after your new baby is born. This is called tandem feeding and some women feel that by breastfeeding both children, it helps the siblings to bond and to reduce the potential for the older child to feel jealous and excluded. If this is something you're considering you may be interested to know that mothers who do tandem breastfeed both their children are less likely to suffer from mastitis than mothers who feed one baby.

If that's not enough to persuade you, and you decide not to tandem feed, then it's better to wean your first baby well in advance of your second baby being born so your first child doesn't feel left out.

Breastfeeding jealousy from your older child

This is how the scenario goes: you've got your new baby home and your older child is touchingly excited and happy as you look at the sleeping baby together. Everything is going just swimmingly. And then the baby wakes up and is hungry and you have to stop doing what you're doing with your child to breastfeed the baby. Your older child feels upset that you are no longer paying them attention, and is intensely jealous of the power the baby has to divert all your attention to it. Why are you holding the baby so close in your arms and smiling at it, when they are not welcome? Suddenly all the happiness and excitement about the new baby disappears and jealousy creeps in.

A lot of women worry about how their older child will react when they start breastfeeding the baby. Some decide not to breastfeed their second baby even though they may have enjoyed breastfeeding their first child, because they worry so much about the effect on their first-born. Or they try and hide the fact that they are breastfeeding the baby from their older child by shutting themselves away in the bedroom whenever they are feeding in the hope that this will protect their older child from unnecessary hurt and resentment towards the baby.

It is undoubtedly true that some older children will initially feel jealous and may take a while to adjust to the new baby being breast-fed. But not breastfeeding your baby, or trying to hide the fact you're doing it is not the answer. In fact most experts agree that letting your child see you breastfeed and allowing them to be involved can actually help your child to feel more bonded to you. Your child will enjoy being asked to help – for example getting a muslin square for the baby, or holding the baby's hand – and being involved will help them not to feel excluded. If they are also allowed to sit close to you while you feed the baby, breastfeeding can become a special time for your older child as well as for you and the baby.

Your child may have plenty of questions to ask about feeding the baby and many young children will want to know whether they were breastfed too. If the answer is yes, then your child may feel better and hopefully less jealous, knowing that they were looked after in the same loving way as the baby.

If you didn't breastfeed your older child, explain that bottle feeding was just as special. You can tell them that it meant that other people were able to feed them with a bottle and how much their dad and other members of the family enjoyed doing this. Part of being a mother to more than one child is realizing that you may not be able to do exactly the same for each one. Don't feel guilty – you do the best you can.

When your toddler asks to breastfeed too

Your child may well ask this question – especially if they have only fairly recently stopped nursing. How you respond to this request is up to you. If you feel comfortable with it you may think it's best to let your child try so that they don't feel rejected and add it to their list of grievances against the baby. The chances are that, having satisfied their curiosity, once will be enough – your child won't like it and won't ask to do it again. On the other hand you may prefer to explain gently to your child that breast milk is only for babies but that children can have drinks the baby can't have. Point out all the other advantages of being 'big' as well, like being able to eat chocolate.

Survival tips for keeping your toddler happy while you are breastfeeding the baby

Prepare a snack box: make the time for feeding the baby be snack time for you and your older child too. It is amazing how your toddler will suddenly decide they are really hungry just after you have sat down to feed the baby. Stock up on healthy snacks and before you sit down to feed, get ready some raisins (it can take small children ages to pick each one up and pop them into their mouth) or some other fruit and/or vegetable sticks and some water for you and your toddler to drink. Remember how thirsty you get when feeding, as well as your toddler. Settle down wherever you're planning to feed the baby and enjoy snacking together.

Keep a basket of special toys for your child to play with only when you are feeding: your child will probably have been given quite a few new toys to celebrate the baby and bringing out this basket whenever you need to feed can make your toddler actually look forward to feeding time. Include in this basket as many activities as possible that can be done without much involvement from you, such as drawing and easy puzzles. Depending on your child's boredom threshold, you'll need to change the contents of the basket fairly regularly, so there's something new to look forward to playing with and which will keep their interest levels up.

Make a Special Time Box: this is a variation on the box of toys for your child to play with while you're feeding, which was recommended to me by family health adviser Ruth Fromow. It's a special box you can make with your child and fill with things you and your older child can do together after your baby has been fed and put down to sleep. You can use any old cardboard box and decorate it together (perhaps while you're feeding your baby) and let your child choose which things they want to do when it's just the two of you.

Reading stories together: this is easily done while feeding and is lovely and bonding. I used to choose two feeding times a day as special story-time feeds. These were the ones when I wanted my older child to feel sleepy – in the early afternoon and at bedtime. The three of us would lie in my bed, my baby feeding on one side and Harry on my other side. Sometimes, instead of reading a book, I'd make up a story, which always included Harry as the central character and Rory, my baby, having super-baby powers, which I think Harry secretly thought Rory might have and actually made him rather proud! If you're too tired to either read a story or make one up, story CDs (audio books) and nursery rhyme CDs are brilliant too.

DVDs and television: these can always be relied on to entertain a child for half-an-hour or so if they're old enough and you don't mind. My children didn't really take any notice of television until they were about three. Making feeding time the only time they are allowed to watch a special programme is one way of limiting the TV and making your child look forward to your baby being fed at the same time.

Sitting down games: the great thing about feeding your second baby is that you are probably much better at being able to do it in almost any position. You probably don't feel that you have to be sitting in the special nursing chair to do it, or lying in your bed propped up with pillows. If you can sit down on the floor with your older child while you're feeding so that you're at the same level, this makes playing games with them much easier. Building bricks, puzzles and Duplo can all be done like this. Word games are good too, such as an easy version of 'I spy' where your child has to spy something which is big, or something which is blue. For children who find it hard to sit down for any great length of time and prefer being more active, you can ask them to find a list of things in the room and bring them to you. This can take up quite a lot of time and be fun. For example: can you find a small thing, a shiny thing, a soft thing, and so on.

Role play: lots of small children like to play at being grown-up and to copy doing whatever you do. Giving your child a doll that is their baby to look after can keep lots of children happy at feeding time. They can feed their baby when you feed yours (though they probably won't want to spend as long doing it as you do). Even boys can enjoy this. My son didn't actually want to spend a lot of time feeding his doll baby, but he did enjoy putting it in its pushchair and rushing around the sitting room with it while I was feeding the baby, and then putting it in a doll cot and rocking it rather ferociously to sleep. Better that than his real baby brother!

Cars and flour: some children are better than others at entertaining themselves and if you're lucky you may have one of those children who can sit happily for hours (well minutes anyway) absorbed in a particular activity. In my experience, girls seem to be better at this than boys and will sit down with some little pots of playdough or colouring things without needing you to entertain them at all. There was only one activity that had the same effect on my boys and this was the cars in the flour activity. If you've never done it before, I recommend you try this for a stress-free feeding time. Sprinkle some flour on a large bread board or tray; then let your child drive his toy cars in the flour and make car tracks and roads. They can make all sorts of patterns and are somehow fascinated by the marks that their different sized cars and wheels make. When the flour gets too messed up you simply smooth it out again for more car tracks. Admittedly it does mean that you have to wash all the flour off the cars afterwards but this is a small price to pay for a peaceful feeding time.

One of the aspects of breastfeeding your second child that is often remarked upon by experts is that the mother has much less time to stare adoringly into the eyes of their baby while they are feeding. So, while doing things with your elder child is important, you also need to remember that feeding your baby isn't just about the mechanics of it, it's also about the emotional contact you have with the baby. If possible, enlist the help of your partner or friends or a babysitter to look after your older child sometimes while you are feeding your baby so you and your baby can both enjoy that exclusive attention you gave your first child. Yes, I know there's always the middle of the night feeds when your older child is hopefully asleep, but as you are probably wishing that you were too, your adoring gaze may just be a little bleary.

Bottle feeding

There are an infinite variety of reasons why mothers choose to bottle feed their babies, either first or second time around and it is still a popular method of feeding. In fact, although 69 per cent of women start off breastfeeding their babies, only 25 per cent are still breastfeeding after six weeks. To put it another way: three-quarters of British women bottle feed their babies after the first six weeks. For many mothers it is because of the positive advantages for them in bottle feeding. The biggest advantage of all is that anyone can feed your baby and it doesn't always have to be the mother's responsibility. The dad and other members of the family – including your first child – can be much more directly involved with feeding the baby so that caring and looking after the baby really can be a shared experience. The fact that it doesn't have to be you waking up to feed the baby several times in the night can make a huge difference to how you cope during the day and this advantage may seem even greater with a second baby when you are more tired and have less time (although many people argue that breastfeeding is quicker because you don't have to spend any time sterilizing bottles or making up the feeds). It also allows you to spend more time with your first child if someone else is feeding your baby at certain times during the day – or even to go out for the evening, if you have the energy.

Bottle feeding for the first time

Most women who have breastfed their first baby go on to do this with their second baby, but if your experience of breastfeeding was traumatic and unhappy, then you may well decide not to put yourself and your second baby through this experience again. You may decide that this time you will bottle feed with formula milk right from the beginning. Or perhaps you have enjoyed breastfeeding, but feel that it would be easier for your older child if you bottle feed the new baby – either so that they don't feel so jealous or because they can join in with the feeding too.

Maybe there are medical reasons why you can't breastfeed this time so that's why you are bottle feeding for the first time.

Although you won't find the mechanics of giving your baby a bottle difficult, it might be worth talking to friends who have bottle fed their babies before. They can give you advice about different types of formula milk and the different brands. Most importantly they will be able to support you in your choice and what you are doing. You need to be confident in your decision, because there are some people who feel so strongly that breastfeeding is the best way to feed your child they might make you feel uncomfortable or guilty about bottle feeding. If you are bottle feeding for the first time because you have to for medical reasons, you may be feeling disappointed. Don't feel guilty and let this spoil your feeding sessions. Remember that bottle feeding can be just as bonding and special as breastfeeding. And if you are less tired as a result, you may well find that you are able to cope better and enjoy your two children more.

Expressing milk

Being able to express your milk so that someone else can feed your baby can be a godsend for mothers – particularly if you have a toddler as well as a baby to look after. If you didn't try expressing with your first baby, give it a go now and see how you get on. The advice is to wait until your baby is four to six weeks old and has become really good at breastfeeding before giving them a bottle – this is so that they don't decide to give up on the breast once they discover how easy it is to suck milk from a bottle.

There are different methods of expressing – all of which make you feel a bit like a cow being milked, but some less so than others. If you can get your hands on an electric pump, this is the quickest and most efficient method and it is possible to hire these from a variety of places, such as your local hospital or the NCT, rather than forking out for the cost of buying one. Alternatively there are hand pumps or, if you've got the time and patience, you can try to do it without any mechanical aid by massaging your breasts with your hands.

Weaning

It doesn't take long before your baby is suddenly old enough to start drinking more than just milk and to join your older child in eating at the table. It takes slightly longer now, of course, than in earlier days when babies started to be weaned on to puréed fruit and vegetables from three months old. Now the official advice is that babies should be exclusively milk fed until they are six months old before starting the slushy solid food.

Despite official advice, with a second baby you may find that they start looking as if they'd like some solid food before they've reached six months. In fact, you may find that your baby starts to grab at food on their older sibling's plate and put it in their mouth. This may not be a sign that they are desperate for more than just milk – it may just be that natural tendency babies have to pick up whatever's within their grasp and put it in their mouth. However, if you do want to try them on solid food before six months, you're advised to check with your health visitor first, who will probably tell you that it's fine to start earlier.

Whenever you decide to wean your baby, you first need to decide how you're going to do it. If your first child is still too small to sit at the table on an ordinary chair, you might want to borrow an extra high chair for your baby so you can feed both children together, instead of in shifts. Alternatively, sit your child on a car booster seat if they don't wriggle too much (otherwise the booster seat falls off the chair).

Next, it's the preparation of the food. If you weaned your first baby on to puréed carrot and mashed banana, you will no doubt have fond memories of chopping, boiling and blending, ice-cube trays and clothes (the baby's and yours) covered with brightly coloured bits of mush and your baby spitting things out in disgust. After a month or so you'll remember how you moved on to mashing things to introduce lumps before you get on to giving your seven to eight month old some finger foods. You can repeat all of these stages with your second baby – spoon of sloppy food in one hand while pretending your forkful of green beans is an aeroplane for your toddler on the other.

Baby-led weaning

If, however, you are not entirely looking forward to this period of feeding your two children, there is an alternative way of weaning your baby, which is becoming increasingly popular particularly with mothers who have second babies. Baby-led weaning, if you haven't heard of it, is when you let your baby feed themselves right from the beginning on finger foods and miss out the puréed food stage. The theory is that puréed food, while necessary for a baby of three or four months, is not so important for a baby of six months who can already hold up their head and sit up with support and whose hand–eye co-ordination has reached the stage where they are able to reach out and grab food in their hands. The fact that your baby has an older sibling to copy means that they will probably be trying to do it anyway.

It certainly makes weaning a much easier process. Instead of having to prepare two completely separate meals for your toddler and baby, you can let your baby have whatever you or your older child are eating cut into pieces that they can easily pick up, such as broccoli spears, pasta, fingers of cheese and sticks of bread, cucumber, cooked carrot on so on. 'Baby-led weaning is the best thing I have ever done,' Nancy, mother of Stan and Albie, told me. 'I didn't have the confidence to do it first time round but it is amazing and they just eat what you eat so it saves buying separate meals.'

Obviously you still have to be careful about what you give them and make sure that they are not eating food they shouldn't be eating (this can be hard when your older child gives your baby a sugary biscuit or a peanut butter sandwich square while you're not looking), but these are foods you probably don't want your toddler eating either. You just have to make sure you have eyes in the back of your head – which every mother does have anyway – and make sure that you never leave either of your children alone when they're eating (so they don't choke on eating too many biscuits). The only other thing to be prepared for is a lot of mess. Babies feeding themselves do not usually do so with great precision! It is quite astonishing how far food can be flung and in what corners bits of wilted apple can hide. But so long as you have some newspaper or a mat under the high chair and a good vacuum cleaner, the worst can be avoided.

Your toddler and food

You may find that feeding your baby is easier than feeding your first child. After all you've fed a baby before so you know roughly what you're doing, but you've never fed your older child at the age they are now before.

Feeding regression

Toddler eating habits can be quite a challenge, especially if your toddler is using food as a way of registering their unhappiness at the arrival of a new baby. You may find that your first child, who has been eating nicely with proper cutlery and eating most of the food on their plate in a grown-up way, suddenly reverts to babyish eating behaviour – so much for the baby learning to eat like their older sibling! Your toddler may want to eat just like the baby. They'll suddenly want to start using their hands to pick up their food and throw the spoon and fork on the floor, or want to drink from a bottle. Instead of feeding themselves they might want you to feed them like you always used to. This is quite common behaviour (see chapter 6 for more about regression and toddler behaviour), very annoying for you, and a great test of your patience, but it is just a phase. The best thing is not to tell them that they should stop behaving like a baby (after all the baby is behaving like a baby and is getting lots of attention for it), but to praise them when they sit nicely and eat well. Give your child the reassurance they need that they are still important to you – which may mean spoon feeding them again for a while – but tell them how impressed you are with them when they feed themselves. If they get lots of good attention for behaving well, then they will, sooner or later, want to behave more like you and less like the baby.

Picky eating

Not all your older child's eating habits are a response to the arrival of a sibling. After the age of one, a child stops growing at such a rapid rate and they don't need quite so much food. If your older child suddenly becomes picky about food or doesn't want to eat very much one day, then this may be simply because they are not hungry. Your older child's eating requirements will change as quickly as your baby's. Here are some tips for coping with your toddler's eating habits:

* Keep on offering your child small amounts of a wide variety of healthy food, and try not to worry too much if one day they only want to eat cereal and the next day they only eat yoghurt and fruit.
* Involve your child with food by cooking with them. Most children enjoy the whole process of mixing and stirring, and rolling out pastry, and are more likely to want to eat food they've been allowed to help make.
* Go to the shops with your baby and child – for short trips – and talk about the different foods you can see.

* Give your child small portions, so that they are not over-whelmed by having too much food on their plate.

Family mealtimes

Mealtimes start to get a lot noisier, messier – and sometimes take a lot longer – once both your baby and toddler have joined in – even if it's just the three of you. And mostly mealtimes do involve just one parent sitting with the children and helping them to eat their lunch or tea, waiting for the other to come home from work to share their adult meal together. But whenever possible I have tried to sit down as a family to eat. My husband always hated the early days of family mealtimes, find-ing the combination of Rory smearing food all over his face and drop-ping what was left on the floor, and Harry – no longer captive in a high chair – getting down every two seconds to get something or other, deeply stressful and frustrating. And it can be! Especially if you mind about table manners and the fact that the meal you have spent ages preparing, to make sure it's got all the essential nutrients your children need, is left on the plate and not eaten. I insisted that we carried on though, partly because mealtimes had always been an important shared family time when I was a child and partly because there were very few times when we all got to sit and be together as a family. Most meal-times were not something we were all present for, but I was deter-mined that if we persevered the children would end up learning how to sit still at the table, that we would be able to have a conversation that consisted of more than 'No, don't put your finger in Rory's yoghurt and draw pictures with it', and that we would all – one day – actually eat the food on our plates. Everything I have ever read about the subject recommends that whenever possible sitting down together as a family at mealtimes is a good idea. These are the reasons given:

* *It increases linguistic ability, i.e. your children will learn a wider range of vocabulary by listening to your adult conversation. Your baby's speaking skills will also improve from hearing their older sibling talking.* This is roughly true – though don't expect too much. As mentioned, the possibility of holding any sort of varied conversation is definitely limited while eating with a baby and toddler. As children get older, the conversation at the table and exchanging of family news and information becomes more important!

* *It encourages children to eat a wider variety of healthy food. Your baby and toddler will be more likely to try different types of food because they have seen their parents eat this food.* There can be few more irritating habits than a child saying 'I don't like that', when they haven't even tried it, so anything you can do to encourage your children to be adventurous with food must be a good thing. And certainly if a child is offered a variety of different foods, and sees you eating them, they do at least have the opportunity to try them even if they don't always make the most of this opportunity. Of course this does mean that you have to offer a wide variety of healthy food – save the tin of spaghetti hoops for when it's just you and the children.

* *The older members of the family act as role models for the younger members of the family at mealtimes. Parents set a good example for their children by demonstrating polite table manners and by eating and drinking healthily.* Children learn by copying – and learning how to eat properly and politely is no exception. By the same token, they can also learn how to eat improperly and impolitely. You can't expect your children to eat lots of healthy fruit and vegetables if you're sitting there eating crisps and chocolate.

* *Sitting down together as a family at mealtimes helps to create a strong sense of being a family.* This is what I've always believed and still do.

Survival tips for stress-free family meals

Involve your baby in family mealtimes right from the start so that it seems a natural thing to do: my sister remembers 'using Joey's car seat buggy as a chair for him indoors so he was at table height and could see us when we were having meals. We felt he was part of the family very quickly rather than always being on another level or surface.' My children, too, have always sat down at a table together to share a meal, so it has been normal for them to do this.

Keep meals simple: you don't want to spend ages in the kitchen preparing elaborate meals no one eats – and which you don't have time to cook anyway. It really doesn't matter what you eat so long as it's vaguely healthy and you're sitting down to eat it together. In fact you don't have to cook at all – preparing sandwiches with some cucumber and carrot sticks is fine if you're all happy to eat them.

Don't provide several different meals for different people: if you tried to take on board every member of the family's likes and dislikes and cook separate meals you will end up feeling like a hotel or restaurant chef taking orders, and very stressed. Most families have at least one meal they all like in common but, if not, provide a wide variety of vegetables to go with the main meal, so that there should be at least one thing that each person will eat.

Turn off distractions: your baby and toddler won't learn how to eat properly if everyone is glued to the television while eating. Similarly, it's hard to have any sort of family conversation while the radio or CD are playing. Turn all these things off, put the answerphone on and switch your mobile phone to silent. It is not at all relaxing to have to jump up and answer the phone the minute you've sat down to eat – but even worse to pretend to ignore the phone ringing, and then wonder who it was who phoned.

Don't expect too much: it is unrealistic to expect your toddler to stay sitting down for too long at the table. Nor is it likely that your baby is going to eat their food without spilling, dropping or smearing something somewhere. Try not to let these things worry you and tell yourself that this will improve as they get older. In the mean time, if your toddler is sitting in a chair that is too big for them and their feet can't touch the ground, provide a small footstool so that they can rest their feet. A toddler whose legs are dangling will more quickly want to jump off their chair to walk about. Once they have finished their meal, you can let them get down – don't make them wait until everyone at the table – including the baby – has finished.

Try not to let family mealtimes become a battleground: remember that the important thing about this mealtime is enjoying being together as a family. If your toddler doesn't want to eat anything on their plate, then maybe they aren't hungry so don't force them to eat it. If your baby is playing with the food on their plate, perhaps that is how they are learning about this new food. Try and focus on the positive things about your children rather than getting too annoyed about small things they will soon grow out of. You want your children (and you) to look forward to eating together and not dread it.

Food for you and your partner

After a busy day of looking after your two children and making sure they are fed properly, it can be quite easy just to want to collapse either straight into bed or on the sofa with a glass of wine, without cooking or eating properly. 'It's one of the great things about having two children,' said my sister-in-law. 'You get so much slimmer than you were before. How can you possibly put on weight when you never get to finish a meal and never stop moving?'

Other friends, though, confessed that because they never had time to eat properly, they just ate junk food – or sometimes comfort food to keep them going – and ended up feeling terrible.

So it is just as important that you eat healthily as it is that your children do. Healthy food will help you keep your energy up, and make it easier to keep going. Finding the time – and the will – to do this is the tricky bit. Here are some tips:

* Have a cooking day at the weekend, when you make large batches of food you can freeze in individual portions to be eaten during the week.
* Pasta and home-made tomato sauce is quick and easy.
* Have a ready supply of healthy snacks – a handful of raisins or other dried fruit and nuts at tea time can give you the energy you need at the end of the day and stop you from eating your children's left-over food.
* If you are eating later than your children, make extra portions of their meal you can reheat for you and your partner. You can always adapt the food slightly to make it more interesting for adult tastes by adding herbs and spices or including, say, a rocket salad to go with the macaroni cheese.
* Don't feel guilty about buying ready prepared meals from the supermarket – there are some healthy ones.
* Share cooking with your partner. If your partner is a potential Jamie Oliver in the making, enjoys cooking and is at home and

able to do it then you are lucky and can just sit back and enjoy being cooked for.

* Keep a supply of take-away menus for emergencies.

Brothers and sisters!
Behaviour, development
and rivalry

'So how is little Johnny finding life with the new arrival?' your friends and family ask after admiring the new baby. This question probably comes hot on the heels of the one about how you're all sleeping.

What we all want and hope to be able to reply is that they love the baby; that they couldn't be happier to have a new brother/sister and are sweetly affectionate; that there are no signs of jealousy at all, and you can't think why everyone makes such a big deal about it. But, in fact, most of us expect our first child to feel at least a bit upset and jealous when the new baby arrives and for their behaviour to change to some degree – while keeping our fingers crossed that it won't. The fact is that the arrival of a new baby in your older child's life is a major change for them, however hard you try to minimize the impact of this change and to keep routines the same, and it is a change that your child may not hugely welcome. After all your child is used to being the centre of attention and a new baby means your child is suddenly expected to share the limelight, not to mention their toys and games, their house and possibly their bedroom. Most importantly of all, they are expected to share you and your love, time and attention. So what should you expect? How will their behaviour change? What behaviour is normal?

Your toddler's behaviour

The first few months of the new baby

The trouble is it is very hard to predict your toddler's behaviour because it is 'normal' for children to react to a new baby in different ways depending on their temperament and their age. Your child might be genuinely happy about their new sibling and enjoy helping you to look after the baby. Equally, your child might not take any particular interest in the baby to begin with. When my son Harry was asked at nursery school what exciting news he had to tell everyone after the birth of his new brother, he thought for a while and then remembered, 'I got a new green jumper. It's really great' – so much for the impression his baby brother had made on him!

Most normal of all, perhaps, is for a child to feel both upset and jealous. The feelings your child might have towards a new baby being brought home have often been compared to the feelings you might have if your husband brought home a new wife – probably not ecstatic! Just as your behaviour has changed because you've now got a little baby to look after as well, your child's behaviour may change too. They may start to do things that you've never seen them do before and are, to say the least, challenging. They are meant to be! What this child is telling you is that they are finding it difficult to share you, that they are feeling insecure and they need reassurance that you still love them.

If your child does feel like this they may show their insecurity and anxiety in a number of ways. In chapter 3 I have talked about things you can do to help your child adjust to the arrival of their new baby, but here is a look at behaviour that is common in children who have just had a new baby brother or sister and are finding it hard to adjust.

● *'I hate the baby'*

Some children, especially if they are a bit older and able to express themselves well, may react by telling you very clearly that they don't want the baby, that they hate it and that you should send it back to wherever it came from. Difficult as this may be to hear, in some ways this very honest expression of how your child is feeling can be helpful, because at least it is out in the open and you can do something about it.

Don't be angry with them for saying it or tell them that they don't really mean it and that they must love their brother or sister, even if you wish they weren't feeling it.

Listen to what they are saying and be sympathetic. Tell them that you understand why they are upset and let them know that it is normal to feel this way (they may be worried about their feelings), but keep on reassuring them by telling them how much you love them.

Take as many opportunities as possible to give them a hug, and be loving and affectionate towards them so that they can see for themselves that the baby doesn't mean you have stopped loving them.

It may also help your child if you tell them you understand how they are feeling because there are some times when you find the baby difficult too. This is not to suggest that you should give your child the impression that you don't like the baby, or that you prefer them to the baby but it may encourage them to want to help you to look after the baby and, by becoming more involved, to feel closer to the baby.

● *'I want to hurt the baby'*

On the whole, most children are not physically aggressive towards the baby – at least not at the beginning. But there may be times when your child pokes the baby to make it cry when they think you're not looking, or gives it a quick pinch or even throws something at it, which can be more dangerous. This is harder to remain calm about.

Move your child away from the baby immediately and tell them that hitting and hurting are absolutely not allowed.

Try to stay calm and not to lose your temper, but do be very firm so they understand this rule.

Keep a watchful eye to make sure it doesn't happen again and, of course, make sure that your child is never left alone with the baby. This is important in the early days even if your child hasn't hurt the baby. (My sister-in-law's daughter Gracie covered her new sister's face in white Tippex dots when she went to answer the phone.) Take some practical precautions like putting up a stair-gate into your baby's room to make it toddler proof. If you see your child about to get upset with the baby, take preventive action. Pick up the baby and distract the older sibling with a song, a toy, an activity or a snack. This avoids you having to constantly tell your child off, which may make your child feel more resentful towards the baby.

If your child is hurting the baby because they are not able to tell you how they are feeling, you need to help them express themselves verbally so they don't need to lash out physically. Saying things like, 'You feel upset when I pick up the baby' may be a great relief for your child when they realize that you do understand how they feel. Tell them that when they are feeling sad or upset they can come to you for a hug, instead of hitting the baby. 'Hugging not hitting' was a much-repeated catchphrase in our house.

You may find it helps if you interpret for the baby. This is what Nell found worked with her son Oscar and second child Molly. She would talk to Oscar as Molly, saying how she, the baby, felt and this helped Oscar to see the baby more as a person with feelings rather than an obstacle to his happiness. You could also try switching it round and asking your firstborn to interpret for you and tell you what they think the baby might be feeling and what they would say if they could.

Sometimes your child may hurt the baby accidentally simply because they don't know what they're doing – for example hugging the baby too tightly, or even prodding the baby out of curiosity rather than malice. Show your child how to handle and touch the baby gently and softly. Even your child who may have deliberately wanted to hurt the baby needs to be shown how to be caring and gentle – and by watching you be tender with the baby as well as with them, they will learn the correct behaviour.

● *'I hate you'*

It is quite common for a child to take out their feelings of anger and bewilderment on you. Particularly if you have had to be in hospital for a few days so that they have been without you, they may want to punish you by either ignoring you or behaving aggressively towards you. They may make a point of ignoring you and not wanting you to do anything with them or for them. Instead they may insist that they only want daddy to help them or any other adult so long as it's not you. This can be particularly hard if you're longing to show them how much you still love them and your child refuses to accept it. However much you find yourself minding that the special closeness you used to share has disappeared, remember that it is a temporary phase, and that you haven't lost your relationship with them forever. If you tell yourself that it is better that they are taking their anger out on you than on the baby this may help too, as may recognizing the benefits of your child developing a close relationship with their dad.

● *'I'm going to be naughty'*

This is perhaps one of the most common reactions a child has to the
arrival of their new sibling, and one of the most exasperating to deal
with as a parent – which it is meant to be. Your child wants you to take
notice of them (and not the baby), and they have an unerring instinct
for behaving in a way that is guaranteed to make sure you do notice
them, even if it means negative attention. Simply doing the opposite
of anything you ask them to do is common, as is more deliberately
naughty behaviour like painting on the walls or the furniture (or themselves), or tipping up the toy-box just after you've tidied everything
away. Sometimes it may seem that trying to remain calm in these situations only makes things worse – your child keeps on finding things to
annoy you and pushing your buttons until you do finally snap. One
friend who had put up with her three year old's naughtiness with
patient calm for as long as she could, finally lost it when her child got
out the scissors and cut off all the fringing on her new leather boots.
It's quite hard to enjoy life with your toddler when they are trying so
hard to make sure you don't. So what can you do?

Give your child as much attention as you can when they are behaving well. Tempting as it may be to make the most of the time when
your child is playing nicely and happily by doing something else (feeding the baby for instance), this is the most important time to stay with
them, play with them and praise them. If you need to feed the baby,
let your child stay with you while you're doing this and play a game
with them or read a book. If the only time you pay your child any real
attention is when they behave badly, it isn't surprising that your child
should choose to carry on doing this.

Be two steps ahead of your child. Think what they might be likely
to do and see how you can prevent it. For example, if your child is a
budding graffiti artist, and might try and paint the carpet while you are

getting the baby up from their nap, keep the paints and felt-tip pens well out of reach, remove scissors from the craft box, etc.

Don't let your child get away with bad behaviour just because you feel sorry for them. Whatever way you decide to discipline your child (time-out, or taking privileges away etc.) make sure that you are consistent, and that your partner is too. If they always get made to sit on the stairs every time they deliberately pour the milk on the floor, or throw toys all over the room, eventually they may decide to give up. They'll have more fun if they don't behave badly.

- *'I love the baby'*

You've probably been on the lookout for jealous or difficult behaviour, but sometimes the opposite type of behaviour can be a problem too. Children who are overly enthusiastic about the baby, never wanting to leave it alone and constantly wanting to pick it up or hold it and hug it must learn not to be too smothering and that the baby needs to be left alone sometimes to sleep. Ask yourself why your child is so keen to be with the baby. It may be out of genuine affection, but it may also be their way of getting your attention, or it may be a way of hiding their true feelings because they don't want to make you sad. Ask your child how they are feeling and make it easier for them to tell you by explaining that it's normal for children to feel upset and that you will understand.

- *'I want to be a baby too'*

It makes perfect sense really. Your child can see how much attention the baby is getting and so wants to be a baby too and starts behaving like one. Suddenly your child wants to be fed by you, even though yesterday they were fighting to feed themselves, they may start to wet the bed and their pants despite being toilet-trained and dry for several months, they may start crawling instead of walking, or crying like a baby all the time and wanting to be carried everywhere. In their eyes, being independent and behaving like a super big boy or big girl means that they don't get any attention, whereas babyish, dependent behaviour does get attention, so that's clearly the way to behave – a sort of 'if you can't beat them, join them', thought process.

Don't panic – this is perfectly normal, if utterly maddening, behaviour. So normal, in fact, that it has a label – 'regression' or regressive behaviour. Your child is taking backward steps instead of moving forwards into independence because they are feeling insecure and want more, not less of you.

Knowing that this is normal behaviour in children with new baby siblings may make you feel less worried, but it doesn't make it any easier to deal with. You are quite busy enough looking after one baby without having to cope with your older child being one as well. But in this case, giving into their demands to be treated like a baby for a little while is probably the most effective way of seeing an end to the behaviour.

* Let your child regress into babyish behaviour for a while. Give them a bottle of baby milk, carry them up the stairs to bed saying 'Ahh, little baby, there, there', grit your teeth and put them in nappies again. It will probably only be for a short time. As soon as your child sees that they can be a baby if they want to be, they will probably get bored and decide to stop.

* Be as patient as you can be and try not to get angry with them for not doing things you know they *can* do. Encouragement is the way forward.

* Don't tell your child to 'stop behaving like a baby' and to do things 'like a big boy or girl'. The point is that they don't want

to be big and they are trying to act like a baby to get your attention.

* Praise your child and give them lots of attention when they do behave more independently and tell them how clever they are being able to do grown-up things. Focus on all the things they can do – not as a big brother or sister but as their own individual achievement.

* Point out all the fun things that a baby isn't able to do, but which your child can do. Give them a sense of pride and achievement in being more capable and bigger.

● *It's not all bad*

It may sound as if the only effect a new baby has on their older sibling's behaviour and development is a bad one but this isn't the case. There is plenty of evidence to show that some children make much more developmental progress after they have become an older brother or sister. These children are motivated to become more independent more quickly, becoming toilet trained easily after the birth, playing independently, getting dressed by themselves and so on. They appear to welcome their role as the older, big brother or sister and are determined to become as grown-up as they can in contrast to the baby. This is mostly down to temperament, but it would also seem that children who have been prepared for the baby before it arrives and where the dad is actively involved in the child care, are more likely to behave like this.

Toddler behaviour a few months later

If you've got through the first few months without any apparent change in your child's behaviour, you'll probably breathe a sigh of relief and assume that your child just isn't the jealous type – or even feel secretly pleased that you've done all the right things to make sure it doesn't occur. So it can come as a bit of a shock when your toddler's behaviour only changes a few months down the line, when your baby is four or five months old or even later. But this is very common. What seems to happen is that when the baby first comes home, it's a bit of a novelty and a curiosity. It doesn't impact on your older child's life too much because your baby spends a lot of time sleeping, and so your child doesn't have to take much notice of it if they don't want to. Added to that, your child may not have realized to begin with that the baby is for keeps and here to stay. It's only after a few months that the realization dawns on your child that the baby isn't going to go away – it's a permanent addition. Not only that but the baby is getting bigger, and being awake more of the time, smiling and sitting up, maybe crawling and moving about – not nearly so easy to ignore as before. It is little wonder that older children start to find things hard at this stage.

How children's behaviour changes at this stage is very similar to before – it's just taken longer to happen. It's still about your child's need for your love and attention, and the advice for how to deal with it remains the same: continued patience, time and attention, and reassurance. But some behaviour changes when they happen later can test you to the limit and be very difficult and upsetting to deal with, as the following stories from parents illustrate:

Mums and dads on behaviour changes:

'For the first few weeks Sarah's behaviour didn't change, but after about three months, she started hitting and biting other children at nursery school, hitting her granny and demanding only mummy. These were isolated incidents but still upsetting at the time; 99 per

cent of the time she was still a happy little toddler ... she grew out of it, but not until the baby was around nine months.'

Alex, father of Sarah, Leo and Annabel

'Stan just started behaving in this hideous negative way – biting me, biting his brother and having massive tantrums. He would wake up in the middle of the night screaming (he had previously been an ace 7 'til 7 sleeper). In fact, he adopted this special scream that was actually just specific to this time. I found it one of the most challenging times of my life because I felt so angry at him for hurting Albie (and me) and actually began to question whether he was a nice child but at the same time I just felt so incredibly sad that my little boy was so hurt and so insecure. He really had been such a lovely, easy-going child until then. There was no quick fix either; it went on for at least six months. We since found out that Stan had hearing problems and actually this accounts for a lot of his frustration at the time. He had an operation when Albie was about six months and emerged a new child with a new-found love of his brother. They are thick as thieves now but looking back I know that at times I thought I would never see this day.'

Nancy, mother of Stan and Albie

In both these cases, the toddlers became aggressive in their behaviour to the baby and other people around them. The natural reaction as a parent is to want to protect the baby and those around you from the violent behaviour; and to feel angry with the older child, as well as sad. Being angry, though, doesn't help the baby or your toddler or you, and can often end up in you feeling guilty and over-compensating your toddler for shouting (by giving him extra hugs or sweets, etc.) and sending confused messages. The advice for dealing with hitting and hurting is the same as when it happens at an earlier stage:

* keep calm but repeat the firm rules about not hurting
* remove your child from the person they've hurt
* encourage your child to talk to you about their feelings
* acknowledge their feelings and tell them that you understand.

Try and find out why your toddler is behaving aggressively. It's natural to assume that it's a reaction to built-up frustration and anger with the baby, but there may be another cause. Perhaps they are tired, hungry or not feeling well – in the case of Stan, it was not being able to hear properly that contributed to his anger. There may be other reasons that are not connected to the baby, which are contributing to why your child is being aggressive.

● *Fears and phobias*

About a third of firstborn children develop a phobia or irrational fear of something at some point in the first year after their sibling is born as a result of insecurity about the baby. This is commonly a fear of the dark, but it might not be – it could be the sound of the lawnmower that suddenly frightens them, or fear of an animal they were previously fine with, or an activity that they now find scary, such as going swimming. Whatever it is, it's important to take your child's fear seriously and not to try and make them face it – by insisting they sleep with the light off for example. The phobia will probably only last for as long as they are feeling anxious about the baby and will pass.

Tantrums and the Terrible Twos

It's worth mentioning that in many families the new baby arrives at just the same time as the older child is entering into the Terrible Twos stage. The fact that your child may be having tantrums, shouting at you and refusing to do anything you ask, or just saying 'no' to everything is common behaviour, whether or not there is a new baby in the house. So don't feel guilty that this behaviour is all your fault for giving them a new baby to deal with. Your child is having tantrums because they find it difficult to deal with their emotions – and because they feel frustrated at not being able to express themselves properly. Children at two say 'no' to everything because they are learning to become independent and are demonstrating their ability to make decisions.

Your baby's development

What's it like for your baby being the second child? And what does it mean for their development that they have an older sibling they must share you with? Many mothers have told me that they have felt guilty about how much less time they spent doing things with their second baby compared with their first. It is, of course, inevitable that you spend less time with your second baby because your time does have to be divided between two. But it is easy to spend so much time worrying about how your elder child is feeling after the new baby is born and making sure they get enough attention that the baby doesn't get their fair share. Victoria, now a mother of four children, agrees. 'A small baby is far easier to deal with than a two year old. The small baby sleeps a lot and can't move, whereas the older one demands much more attention. Nancy turned out to be such an easy baby (compared to Rose) that I think we took her completely for granted and contrary to expectation showered far more attention on Rose.' This was true in my case, too. My second child Rory was an easy baby (or was that because I was a more experienced mother?), so he often just got moved around from room to room in his Moses basket, or plonked in his bouncy chair when he was a bit older, to wherever Harry was playing while I concentrated on keeping Harry amused and entertained. Rory as a baby didn't demand attention apart from when he needed feeding, whereas Harry did and so he got it.

Less anxious about development

It is also true – and sometimes another thing to feel guilty about – that I was far less concerned about Rory's growth and development. With Harry I would pore over baby books to see what he should be doing when and make sure that he was hitting those developmental milestones. I'd pop to the baby clinic every week and compare notes with other mothers and try not to mind too much if their baby pulled their right ear before mine did. With Rory I lost track of all these things. It wasn't that I didn't care about his development or his growth but I could see that he was putting on weight – I didn't need to get him weighed every other second. And I knew that Rory would do the things he was meant to – he would roll over onto his tummy, he would sit up and learn to crawl – and that he would do them in his own good time. Whether he did them this week or next week was immaterial. If anything, I rather hoped that he would not learn to do these things too quickly. I knew what lay in store once he could master these skills – and that a mobile, crawling Rory was going to pose a whole set of new challenges with his older brother that I didn't relish. I learned, too, that I loved Rory's babyhood – I was in no hurry for him to grow up too fast, as I had been with Harry.

I don't think this lack of ambition for Rory's development held him back. Second babies can often benefit from having mothers who are more relaxed about their progress, and what they may miss out on in terms of undivided attention from their mother is amply made up for in time spent watching their older sibling (see below). However, there are some areas of a second baby's development that can be adversely affected by the presence of an older brother or sister, and that it's worth being aware of.

Look at your baby and communicate with them

It sounds obvious, but recently there have been some worrying statistics about language delays occurring in children because mothers have not spent enough time looking at their baby and communicating with them. With a toddler to look after, most mothers find that they spend much less time actually looking at their baby – unlike with your first child when you may have spent hours gazing in wonder at their face. So while you're remembering to keep your older child entertained in order that they don't feel excluded as you feed the baby – don't forget that you need to look at your baby while you're feeding them too. Having one-to-one time with your baby is just as important as it is for your toddler. You may be able to hold a verbal conversation with your older child, but your baby will be learning to communicate with you by looking intently at your face and taking in your different expressions. They need to look at you and you to look at them to learn and develop.

Don't over-protect your baby

Another potential problem for second babies is that they are given less floor time – both before and after they learn to crawl – because parents are trying to protect them from their older sibling. So instead of being put on the floor on their tummies, they are put in a bouncer or a baby-seat, or constantly carried on their mother's hip to keep them out of harm's way. The reason this matters is because babies need this floor time to develop their physical skills. Being put on the floor, babies learn to strengthen their muscles, which will help them to learn to roll over, sit up and crawl. Once they have learned to crawl, they need to be given the freedom to explore and discover the world around them – that's how they learn. Constantly picking them up and restricting their free-dom of movement – so they don't destroy their older sibling's brick tower and get hit over the head for example – may, in the long term, delay their learning and development. To avoid this problem try and find safe areas for your older child to play with their toys without being disturbed – in their bedroom, for instance, or on a higher level such as a table – so that the baby can be allowed to explore at ground level.

Give your baby new experiences

Most mothers with a second child cope by developing very organized routines. And this is important for developing both children's sense of security and for giving a structure to each day. But while predictable routines are helpful – essential in fact – it's also important to remem-ber that children need to have new and different experiences too to keep them interested and to help them to learn. If they do exactly the same thing each day, go to the same places and play with the same things, it becomes boring. So if you always go to the park in the morn-ing, try going a different route so you can see different things or go to a different park altogether once in a while. If your baby plays with the same toys every day that were bought for your first child, think how you can give them different toys to play with occasionally – try rotating them, or join a toy library or swap toys with friends from time to time. At this age, too, toys don't need to be purpose bought – everyday objects such as plastic cups or cotton reels can be just as entertaining for your baby. Injecting a bit of variety into your baby's routine and providing new stimulus not only helps your children's development but will make your life a bit more interesting too.

Do some things just for the baby

Many second children spend much of their first year being taken to their older sibling's activities, and just fit in with the life that has been designed for and centres on your first child. They sit in their car seat while the older brother or sister does their music/gym/dance class or they get taken to their nursery school and taken back home again, etc. And this is not necessarily a problem – your baby will learn a lot just by watching and listening to their sibling's activities – it's all new to them. But even if your baby does fit easily and happily into your first child's routines, it's important to start thinking of doing some things that are either just for your baby (baby massage, baby swimming or music) when your first child is occupied at nursery or playing at a friend's house, or activities where both your children can actively participate – baby and toddler groups, or soft play centres, etc.

Keep a record of your baby's development

You've probably got a record of *everything* your first child did when they were a baby, not to mention hours of video footage and hundreds of photographs, so don't forget to keep a record of your new baby's growth and development too. You may think you'll never forget but you do – it needs to be written down because when they get older they *will* ask you when they first smiled, and how old they were when they started to crawl and what their first word was. And if you can't tell them because you forgot to record the momentous event, when you've got a whole stack of neatly filled-in child health records and perfectly captioned photograph albums for your first child, you are going to feel guilty. It doesn't matter how much you try and explain that you just didn't have the time to do it with two children, the fact is that you found the time to do it for your first child and your second child may easily feel they don't matter to you as much.

Learning from their older brother or sister

There may be a few issues about being a second child that make things harder for your baby's development, but there are some advantages too. One of the biggest advantages a second baby has over a firstborn child is that they have an older sibling to learn from. Babies and young children are copycats – they'll watch what their big brother or sister is doing and will try it out for themselves. It may be making a funny face, or making different sounds and noises – second children often learn to talk earlier than first children. Your crawling baby will watch their older brother or sister build a tower of bricks – and learn not only how to build the tower themselves but also what happens when you swipe at it with your fist – it falls down and you upset your sibling! Later on, your second baby may learn how to sing nursery rhymes from their sibling and they may learn to read and write much earlier than your first child did as they watch their older brother or sister learning to read and write with you. (They may also learn some language and behaviour from your first child that you'd rather they didn't!)

Your second child may indeed think their older brother or sister is absolutely amazing for all the things he or she can do that they can't, and be full of hero-worshipping adoration, smiling every time they come into a room, clapping their hands in excitement and being sad when they are not there. This can be true even if the older child takes no notice of them or is sometimes horrid to them. But for most firstborn children, even if they do find their younger brother or sister annoying and hate them some of the time, being hero-worshipped for their advanced skills is a wonderful confidence boost and very flattering.

Your second child has the advantage of being able to learn from their older brother or sister's mistakes too. They can see what happens when a certain course of action is taken. An example might be the older child deciding to take sweets from the cupboard without asking before lunchtime. Your second child will learn (1) where the sweets are kept, (2) how to climb onto the chair to reach the cupboard and (3) what happens when mum finds out. They can then decide for themselves whether it's worth copying this behaviour or not!

Birth order and your child's character

The nature versus nurture debate has always fascinated me. Are my children the way they are because of what they've inherited genetically from me and their dad or is their behaviour down to the way we've brought them up? A bit of both probably, but all sorts of external things can influence your children's character and behaviour, including, it's believed, where they come in the family – whether they are firstborn, second born, an only child or the youngest in a family of nine. Here are some examples of what are thought to be typical character traits of first and second-born children.

Firstborn child: the elder child has to bear the full weight of their parents' expectations and desires. For this reason they are often conscientious children who not only try hard to please, but may also be very successful and high achieving. They can also be bossy (used to bossing their younger siblings around) and may be a bit neurotic or anxious, particularly if they feel the stress of being the elder child becomes too much. As a parent it's important not to make your first child feel too pressured by your hopes and expectations for them.

Second-born child: especially if they are also the youngest member of the family, the second-born child is often used to being the baby of the family, getting a lot of attention and sometimes being a bit spoilt. At the same time, because second-born children have always had an older sibling around them, they are thought to be more social, to enjoy having people around them and be great fun. Second-born children are also thought to benefit from their parents' experience with their first child by being more relaxed, laid-back and independent. Second children are often given more freedom to do things, and get the opportunity to try things out earlier than their older brother or sister (much to their older sibling's annoyance!). Finally, your second child may be more of a rebel and a risk taker than your first child, because a second-born child has something to prove, and needs to carve out their own niche in the family.

Of course these character traits may not be evident in your children at all – but it's worth thinking about how you treat your children differently because of where they come in the family.

Playing together

The best thing of all is when your second child learns not from passively watching their older brother or sister but by actively doing things with them. And when you watch your two children engaging and interacting with each other and playing together at last, you feel it was all worth it. One of the best sounds you can hear as a mother is that of your children giggling and laughing at the same funny thing. This is what you hoped for your two children: that they would learn to enjoy each other's company, they would make each other laugh and that they would entertain each other and become friends.

Although the difference of ability between your baby and toddler is particularly marked in the baby's first year, there are still plenty of things they can do together and play together, which can be enjoyable for both. When the baby is tiny your older child can interact with the baby by bringing toys to play with, making conversation with and funny faces at the baby, playing finger rhyming games, showing them books.

Once the baby can sit up, but before they can move, they are perfect for children who like to do dressing up and play games of pretend. Your child can practise their directorial skills (not to say bossy ones) by instructing the baby: 'You be the dwarf who sits there, I'll be the beautiful princess' – or at least that's what I used to do with my little sister. Your baby is a built-in captive audience for an older child who likes to perform, whether it's singing or dancing – they may not participate much, but they'll be taking it all in. And you may find that your baby smiles first not at you, but at their older sister or brother. As the baby gets older and is able to do more things, opportunities for shared play increase. Your child can play peek-a-boo with the baby to gurgles of delight, games of chase the crawling baby can start, and games of hide and seek. By the time your baby is about ten months old, they can hold a fat crayon and do art with their older sibling.

When they don't play together

It may not always be easy to get your baby and toddler to play well together and there will certainly be times when they want to do completely different things or want to be on their own. If your older child doesn't want to do things with the baby, they shouldn't be made to. At the same time, your older child does have to understand that the baby needs you to play with them too. If you want to be doing quiet games with your baby while your older child wants you to do noisy, active things outside it can be hard to know what to do. Use the time when one or other is asleep or at nursery to play with your children on an individual basis.

The following chart offers some advice on how your toddler can help your baby's development at different stages. Babies develop at different rates, of course, so this is only an approximate guide to what your baby may be doing when.

Your baby will love all the attention they receive from their older sibling. How much your toddler enjoys playing with their younger brother or sister will depend to a large extent on their temperament!

How your toddler can help your baby's development

Age of baby (months)	Your baby	Your toddler
1	Even in the first month your baby can recognize certain voices and turn towards ones they recognize. Higher-pitched voices are more easily understood.	Get your child to talk to the baby softly and tell them to watch out for the baby turning towards them when they recognize the child's voice. Your child's higher-pitched voice may be particularly interesting to your baby.
	Your baby can see but not very well, focusing best on things that are 20–25 cm (8–12 inches) away. The baby prefers faces to look at rather than other shapes and will hold your gaze intently.	Show your child how to put their face close enough to the baby so the baby can focus on your child. If your child moves their hand from side to side, the baby will follow it with their eyes.
	Your baby has a strong reflex grasp.	Let your baby hold onto your child's little finger. The baby will grasp it tightly. You ca tell your child how the baby likes them so much the baby doesn't want to let go.

Age of baby (months)	Your baby	Your toddler
2–3	Your baby will start to smile around now.	Encourage your child to smile at the baby – they may be rewarded with the baby smiling back for the first time. A wonderful feeling!
	Your baby can see more clearly now and will reach for dangling objects.	Your child might enjoy finding toys to show the baby and demonstrate the noise that toys like rattles or squeaky books make.
	Your baby will repeat sounds like 'ooo' and 'ahhh'.	Hearing your child's voice will fascinate your baby. Encourage your child to talk and sing to the baby.
4–6	If you put your baby on the floor, they can lift their head go degrees, and will roll over if put on their tummy. By month six your baby may be able to roll backwards and forwards.	See if your toddler will lie down on their tummy too, to look at the baby at the same level.

Age of baby (months)	Your baby	Your toddler
4–6 (cont.)	By month six your baby will be able to sit with minimal support.	Get your child to practise their counting skills while your baby is learning to sit up – the game is to count how long the baby can sit up for before falling back onto cushions!
	Your baby can see across the room and will copy facial expressions.	Your child may enjoy making funny faces for your baby and see if they try to copy them.
	Your baby can make sounds of two syllables and will babble away a lot of the time.	Carry on talking to the baby and see if the baby will repeat the sounds your child makes.
	Your baby will be fascinated by their fingers and toes.	Show your child how to play finger rhymes with the baby, such as This little piggy and Round and round the garden, on the palm of the baby's hand.

Age of baby (months)	Your baby	Your toddler
7–9	Your baby will be on the move, starting to crawl or bum shuffle and taking an interest in everything they find, putting objects in their mouth to see what they feel like. Your baby will be interested in quite small objects too and will be able to pick them up.	Prepare your child for the fact that they may find things a bit difficult once the baby is crawling. Explain that the baby may be able to destroy their towers or pick their cars and trains up off the tracks – not deliberately to be annoying, but because it's interesting. Show your child how to distract the baby by giving them a different toy to play with. Explain to your toddler that it's important not to leave small objects on the floor, like marbles or beads, which the baby could pick up and choke on.
	Your baby will be increasingly interested in how things happen – and as your baby's memory improves they will remember what is likely to happen if you do one thing – it makes another thing happen.	If your child is old enough to play peek-a-boo, your baby will find this very exciting around now and laugh a lot.

Age of baby (months)	Your baby	Your toddler
7–9 (cont.)	Dropping objects and looking for them will be endlessly fascinating for your baby.	If your child is very patient they can participate in the baby's favourite game of dropping things from the high chair and waiting for them to be picked up so the baby can drop them again (your child is the picker upper). Your baby will play this for hours, though your older child may not find it so much fun.
10–12	Your baby will be much more mobile now – can crawl with ease and climb up and down stairs. They will be able to stand if someone holds their hand and may even take their first steps – nearly a toddler now. Your baby can cruise around furniture too.	There are lots of games your toddler can play with the baby now. Hide and seek is a good one – your toddler hiding behind the sofa and then reappearing to surprise the baby. The baby may be startled at first and then burst into fits of laughter. A slightly longer game involves you hiding with the baby while your toddler/preschooler finds you.

Age of baby (months)	Your baby	Your toddler
10–12 (cont.)	Your baby can clap their hands and wave bye bye, and bang two objects together.	Try clapping games and action rhymes, such as Incy wincy spider, and Five little ducks, all together.
	Your baby will 'dance' to music.	Put the music on and your baby and toddler can dance together.

Sibling rivalry

At some point, probably even during your baby's first year, you will see the first stirrings of sibling rivalry and jealousy in your second child. To begin with it may be something as simple as your ten month old wanting the toy his sister has got. He tries to get it and he cries in frustration and anger when she won't let him have it. As your baby becomes more verbal as well as physically active, the fighting and arguing may begin in earnest. 'It's mine!', 'It's not fair', 'I hate you', 'Give it back', 'She hit me'. As a parent of two children, these phrases may become very familiar to you!

One minute your children are best friends, the next they are the deadliest enemies. It can be exhausting to keep up with. It can also be very hard to cope with if it happens on a daily basis, particularly as we all want our children to love and be kind to each other and for the family we've created to be a happy one. You may see it as a failing on your part if the children fight all the time. It isn't. The degree to which your children get on will depend a great deal on their personalities. Brothers and sisters can be completely different characters and this may help them to get on or it may mean that they clash all the time. But while sibling rivalry is very normal, there are things you can do to help make life easier for all of you and help your children to get on.

Respect your children as individuals: despite the fact that your children share 50 per cent of their genes, they may be very different – in the way they look, the way they behave, what they like and what they don't like. Your first child may be very confident and outgoing, while your second child may be more shy and retiring. One may be very artistic, while the other may prefer more physical activities. Give them opportunities to discover what their individual talents and skills are. Sometimes a second child may deliberately choose different hobbies and interests to focus on in order to avoid competition and comparison with their sibling. In any event, enjoying your children's differences – as well as their similarities – without directly comparing them, will help your children feel valued for the individuals they are, rather than measuring themselves in terms of how they compare to their sibling. Encouraging your children to do well in different areas also helps to avoid competition between them. And if you ever get asked the question 'Who do you love the most?', rather than telling them that you love them both the same, tell them that you love each of them for the very special, unique person that they are.

Don't show favouritism: even if you do find one of your children easier to get on with than another, it's really important you don't show it. Comments, such as 'Why can't you be as tidy as your sister?' or 'Sit nicely at the table like your brother', will do nothing to endear the less favourably compared brother to his sister. Naturally enough, the unfavoured child will feel resentment and it doesn't make things easier for the favoured child either in the long run who may feel guilty, or nervous that their 'status' won't last. But not showing favouritism doesn't mean that you have to do exactly the same for one as you do for the other. While you should make sure that your children get equal amounts of attention it is almost impossible to ensure that they always get exactly the same things as each other. Just make sure that you give each child what they need – they are different and their needs will be too.

Make sure your children have things to do: one of the reasons your children may argue a lot and get into fights may have less to do with resentment and more to do with needing something to do. Fighting often escalates when children are bored. As the saying goes, 'the devil makes work for idle hands', so make sure your children's hands are busy and they are using them to do something creative rather than destructive.

Teach your children to respect each other's possessions: sharing is something that most young children find difficult to do so you need to be careful not to expect too much too soon. If you force your children to share everything, resentment may easily develop. Allow your children to have their own things – which they can keep in a separate box – and which they don't have to share. If your older child outgrows a toy, it's much better if you ask them before giving it to their younger sibling – and if they say no, respect this. Try asking again a bit later and the answer will hopefully be different. Praise your children whenever they do share their things nicely.

Encourage your children to care for and look after one another: if one child is hurt or sad suggest the other one gives their brother or sister a cheering up hug or a kiss. Reward your children with lots of praise whenever they show kindness to one another.

Minimizing fighting

Show by example! If you and your partner are always fighting, then it is more likely your children will too. If you hit your children, then you are sending the message that hitting is acceptable. You need to have firm rules about not hitting and hurting – for all the family – and be consistent.

When you hear the first sound of an argument developing, try not to rush in immediately and put a stop to it, unless you think it's becoming violent. It is better if your children can work things out for themselves. If you are called in as a referee, then be prepared to listen to both sides but try not to judge. You can make suggestions – recommend taking it in turns for example – but ask them to listen to each other too and see if they can solve the problem between each other.

Don't always assume that the one who is crying is the victim. Sometimes the victim has needled their brother or sister and pushed them until their patience finally snaps and they lash out.

Help your children deal with feelings of anger by accepting and understanding the feelings and giving them a way of dealing with it. If your child needs an outlet for their feelings of aggression, give them a pillow to punch. Other children may find that drawing a picture of how they feel helps them to feel better.

The benefits of sibling rivalry

It can be hard to think of the positive side of your children arguing the whole time – most of us would much rather our children didn't do it. However, some good can come out of it. A healthy rivalry can spur children on to do their best, and to achieve their potential. Your children will learn to stand up for themselves, how to deal with their feelings and how to be independent. They will hopefully learn to become more tolerant and patient too, understanding that people may hold different points of view. Skills of negotiation, problem-solving and compromise may be a result of endless arguments, finally resolved, between siblings – all of which will help your children in their life outside the family and with friends.

All of this may take time. Remember that the way your children feel about each other may change as they grow and develop. Your toddler and preschooler may fight constantly while they are both still at home, but then when your elder one starts school they may be ecstatic to see each other in the afternoon. Perhaps the moment of real friendship begins when both your children are at school, and they can talk about their teachers, their lessons, and maybe your older child will keep an eye out for their younger sibling at play time. Or it may not happen till later that your children decide that they like each other's company after all.

A shared childhood and shared family experiences can make the friendship between siblings – at whatever stage it happens – the strongest friendship of all, one that lasts them throughout the whole of their lives.

SEVEN

Going out – with your children, with your partner and for yourself

Just before my second child was born I tried to remember what it was like having a newborn baby. What stuck in my mind most clearly was how long it took me to do everything and I laughed when I remembered my early attempts to get out of the house just for a simple trip to the shops – it could take all morning. That wouldn't happen again, I thought, now I knew what I was doing. Well, I was wrong. Doing anything with a baby and toddler takes more than twice as long as it does with one child, and getting out of the house and going places is no exception, as I quickly discovered the first time I tried to venture out with the two of them after Rory was born. The logistics of going on an outing which includes one nervous mother, one attention-seeking toddler and one new baby, is enough to daunt even the most intrepid traveller!

The thing is that where you might have decided not to venture outside for weeks after your first baby was born, you probably have to go out much more quickly after your second. As one mother said to me: 'You just have to get on with things second time round. No time for mooching around in pyjamas. You can't stay in – you still have to take your toddler to the playground.' Unless you've got someone else who can take your toddler out to their nursery/playgroup/music class, you have to go too with the baby.

Of course, some people do arrange for a helper to take their toddler to their activities, or to look after both children while they go shopping, go to the bank, etc. Some mothers I spoke to found that going out with two children was so stressful that they would rather stay at home with their children where they were safe, and wait to do their shopping, etc. when their partners got back home in the evening or at weekends. But the problem with not going out and staying in all day is that unless you've got lots of space both inside and out where you live, you get cabin fever. More than ever with two children you need to get out in order to keep you all sane.

The best way of getting out with two children

If your first child is not old enough to walk everywhere, you need to decide the best method of ferrying two children around when on foot. Do you stick with your single buggy and use a sling or baby carrier for the baby? Or should you use your single buggy for the baby and attach a buggy-board for your toddler? Or do you swap your single buggy for a double one so both your children are safely strapped in? Here's some advice from parents who've been there!

Mums and dads on getting out and about with two children

'Get one of those BabyBjörn baby carrier things (that you wear), then a double buggy, then a single with a buggy board: for me the main thing was getting both of them to walk a.s.a.p. (I mean the mile or so to school) as the pushing two of them up the hill each day would have been a killer.'

Sheena, mother of Tom and Belle

'My biggest regret was not getting a double buggy. I really thought that I didn't need one and really didn't want yet another thing cluttering up the house. This was very foolish of me. Stan was two years and four months when Albie was born; that is too young to walk everywhere! I used to put Albie in the sling and push Stan but that was hard on my back and I think fuelled Stan's jealousy. You live and learn hey?'

Nancy, mother of Stan and Albie

'Living in a village, a buggy one in front of the other is easier. I have a Jane Powertwin and it is great.'

Shellie, mother of Blake and Brinley

'I found having a papoose [sling] and a buggy easier for me. Probably because Oscar had reflux and needed to be upright!'

Vicci, mother of Olivia and Oscar

'My double buggy was a Maclaren and it was a life saver – I found it much easier to walk everywhere than to load up the car.'

Clare, mother of Issy, Anna, Cecily and Zac

'Phil&Teds [is the best double buggy] I think. It seems to be the only one which is good for toddler and baby and that's easy to steer and pack away.'

Chloe, mother of Oliver and Elise

'We bought a massive Jane buggy. Didn't use it much though. Get dad to carry your eldest, or get a buggy-board, or bike, or scooter.'

Alex, father of Sarah, Leo and Annabel

So there's no definitive answer. Different solutions suit different people depending on where you live (busy streets or bumpy lanes) and also your toddler. If you have a child who is likely to run off at a moment's notice to look at the beautiful bear in the window on the other side of the road, then something to keep your child safely strapped in is essential for your own sanity as well as your child's survival. If, on the other hand, your child is good at holding your hand and not running off, then relying on a buggy-board for the occasional ride may suit you better. Here's a bit more information about the various options you may find worth taking into account when making your decision.

Double buggies

There are a huge number of different styles to choose from to fit your circumstances and your purse – prices can range from anything between £200 and £600 – but only two basic types to choose from: the tandem (one seat in front of the other); or the twin (seats side by side). Either will seem incredibly bulky, heavy and difficult to manoeuvre at first compared to pushing a single buggy, although some are much easier than others. The trick is to find the one that most suits your requirements – for example a heavy double buggy is no good if you live in a flat up a lot of stairs as Helen, mother of Joe and Ella found: 'We were living in a second floor flat when Ella was born and I hadn't really taken on board what a physical strain it would be having two children. Having a double buggy was a nightmare from that point of view. When we got in, I'd have to carry each of the children up individually – Joe was going through a stage of insisting on being carried everywhere – and then finally drag the double buggy up, clunking on every step. After a few months I was a physical wreck!'

Apart from the weight of your buggy, you also need to think about storage space and where and how you'll store a double buggy in the house and in the boot of the car. Some double buggies take up much less space than others, and the ease of folding them varies hugely too. You can also get three-wheeler, all-terrain double buggies, which are great if you live in the countryside and spend a lot of time walking, but tend to be considerably heavier and take up more space.

● *Tandem buggies*

With one seat in front of the other, tandem buggies are the same width as single pushchairs, and so are much easier to fit through narrow doorways. One seat is usually specifically designed for newborn babies, being padded and able to recline fully so that the baby can lie flat. The other seat, at the front, is more upright and more suited to toddlers up to the age of five. Some tandems can be bought as a single buggy and converted to a double when you need it.

Advantages include:

✳ as the toddler sits in the front, it is more difficult for them to disturb the baby

* the seats tend to be wider than those on a twin pushchair
* can fit in narrow spaces.

Disadvantages include:

* can be less stable than twin pushchairs
* the length can be a problem, particularly in small lifts (although some tandems stack your children, so the toddler sits over a lying down baby)
* folding mechanism can be a bit difficult
* heavier and bulkier, even when folded
* more difficult to steer and manoeuvre.

● *Twin buggies (side by side)*

Look for a model where both seats can work independently, so both children can sleep or one can be sat up, etc. Some twin buggies are much lighter than others so it's worth trying them out. It's also possible to get three–wheeled, all-terrain versions.

Advantages include:

* your children sit next to each other, which avoids potential arguments about who gets to sit in the front later on
* tend to be lighter than tandem buggies
* more stable.

Disadvantages include:

* very wide, so may not fit through all doorways – important to check beforehand that it can fit through yours
* seats can sometimes be too narrow in an attempt to reduce the overall width.

Baby carriers/slings

If you didn't have one of these for your first baby, I strongly recommend considering buying or borrowing one for your second, even if you also decide to have a double buggy. Relying on a sling to carry your baby around all the time may put a lot of strain on your back, but they are ideal for short trips out when a double buggy might be impractical or just too much hassle. They are also wonderful for carrying your baby around inside the house, giving you the use of both hands to do things with your toddler, and for soothing fretful babies to sleep. Some toddlers may feel a bit jealous of the baby being carried so close to you, but this problem is usually offset by the fact that you are able to do more things with the toddler.

There are lots of different baby carriers to choose from, which allow you to carry your baby upright in front, or on your hip or lying crossways. Talk to friends and see what they recommend, and try one out, but with a toddler to look after as well it's particularly important to choose one that is easy to put on and take off. Some will allow you to feed your baby discreetly while they're in the sling, and this can be invaluable.

Buggy-boards/kiddy-boards

If your first child is quite good at walking most of the time but sometimes needs a rest, you may find that a buggy-board is a cheaper and less bulky option for you than buying a double buggy. The boards are recommended for children aged between two and four, and most of them will fit onto the back of most buggies, though do check first.

Most children seem to love the chance of going for a ride on a buggy-board, but it's worth seeing if your child does like it before buying one. One mother told me that her daughter simply refused to go on it, despite bribing with chocolate, so she had to return it, unused, to the shop. Other mothers have warned that it can be hard work pushing a child on a buggy-board, especially uphill, and that the added weight on the back of the buggy makes the buggy more likely to topple backwards when going downhill. It can take a bit of practice before managing to push your child on a buggy-board without hitting your leg on the board too. The other obvious disadvantage compared to a double buggy is that your child does have to stand up all the time – you can't strap your child into a seat and hope that they will fall asleep while you push them around.

Getting out of the door

This really does take much longer than you might think possible. Here's a summary of what you have to do:

* Get both children suitably dressed – easier in the summer when you don't have to find so many clothes, but you do have to remember sun hats and sun cream – without the baby crying because they had been asleep and didn't like being woken up, and without the toddler having a tantrum because they don't want to wear what you want them to wear to prevent them from getting a cold and passing it on to the baby.
* Get yourself suitably dressed – this means not wearing pyjamas especially now Tesco seems to have banned the wearing of nightwear in their supermarkets – and finding a clean front-opening shirt for discreet feeding if necessary and locating trousers or a skirt that will fit, but aren't maternity ones because you've been wearing maternity clothes for six months now and

you're no longer pregnant and can't bear the thought of wearing them ever again.

* Pack a nappy bag and make sure you've got everything you need for every eventuality for two children (nappies, wipes, muslin, cream, changes of clothes for the baby; toy, book, snack, drink and change of clothes for toddler; keys, purse, phone, water – and possibly chocolate just in case – for you; and Rescue Remedy for everyone in the event of dire emergency plus more chocolate).

* Remember how the shop assistant demonstrated that you open the new double buggy without breaking it. Apparently it's so easy that you can do it with one arm while holding your baby under your other. So why can't you get it to open using both hands?

* Open the buggy and strap in the baby.

* Strap in the toddler and give them a book to look at.

* Unstrap the toddler and take them to do a wee before strapping them in again.

* Open the door and panic that the twin double buggy you had carefully measured won't in fact fit through the door.

* Get through the door and then realize that it's started to rain and you need to fit the rain cover on. Locate the rain cover, finally attach it and then realize it's Wednesday and the trip you'd planned to the library is a waste of time because it's closed.

A bit of an exaggeration, perhaps, but not much.

Mums on getting out of the door:

'Allow at least half-an-hour to get out of the door and make sure you've fed the baby first!'

Clare, mother of Issy, Anna, Cecily and Zac

'Don't be in a rush. It's always stressful trying to leave the house in a hurry . . . And get people to come to you if you can, from time to time!'

Chloe, mother of Oliver and Elise

Where to go and what to do with your baby and toddler

From the very early days after Rory was born, I found getting out of the house instantly made everyone feel better. It didn't particularly matter whether we had anywhere to go or not – the movement of the buggy wheels would always send the baby to sleep or stop him from crying, and having new and different things to look at interested my quickly bored, active toddler. While they were happy, I was too; I could relax and just enjoy being outside. We might feed the ducks and look at the willow trees overhanging the stream or walk to the railway line and time it to be there when a train went by, or just go to the swings and slides in the park. Gentle, easy daily walks.

Trips to the shops

Sometimes of course we had an outing with a purpose – food shopping being the main one. Even if you do your weekly shop online, there is always something you've forgotten, or suddenly run out of, or you want to buy fresh fruit and veg, and choose it for yourself. But shopping trips with two children are one of the most dreaded outings for many mothers. The prospect of tantrums if your toddler isn't allowed a sweet, and the stares of disapproving shoppers as you try and reason with them while calming your now awake and screaming baby are too dreadful to contemplate. Here are some tips for surviving the shops and making the ordeal a little easier:

* Feed both children before you go. Your baby will be more likely to sleep through the whole outing and your toddler is less likely to demand food out of hunger. (They'll probably still want the food, but you don't have to feel guilty that they actually need it.)

* Keep shopping trips as short as possible and limit what you put on your list. If you actually need more, either do two separate trips or get your partner to buy the extra items on the way home.

* Carry your baby in a sling and put your toddler in the trolley seat, or bring a blanket to cushion the trolley baby seat.

* Make a picture shopping list with your toddler before you go. Tell them to look out for the things on the list and tell you when they spot them. Allow your toddler to put the non-breakable things in the trolley.

* Tell your toddler they are allowed to choose one treat to have at the end of the shop – if they know they can have something, hopefully this will stop them pestering you for too much else while you go round the shop.

* Don't spend too much time putting food away the minute you get home if your children need you. So long as the frozen stuff gets put in the freezer, the rest can wait until later.

Activities

'If you are lucky enough to have bright children, do not assume they will occupy themselves. They are much harder to deal with as toddlers and need you to talk to them and explain the world as you manage the baby, the dishes, the dinner, the baking, the car wash, the shopping, the swings and the late arrival of Daddy. They will likely need stimulation throughout their waking hours.' This was the advice Gayle, mother of Theo, Katia and Adelaide, gave to me, and I agree with her, though it's not just bright children who need stimulation. All children need to be talked to and engaged with, by all family members.

You've probably already got your first child engaged in various activities and your second will get used to being a spectator at their brother or sister's music class, gym club, friend's house and so on. However, as your baby gets older you need to find places to go and things you can do which allow both of them to take part. Some of the most popular suggestions from the mothers I have spoken to include:

Soft play: as Sarah, mother of Anna and Luke, says: 'I used to go there every week. I'd sit with Luke in the ball pond area and he'd spend ages just picking up the balls and throwing them or just patting them. He loved it. Anna would go off with her friend and I knew they were safe because everything's padded. They knew where I was so they'd come back and tell me what they'd done and then run off again.' If you can go with a friend it's even better, so one of you can sit with the babies and the other one can scramble over foam blocks to play with the toddlers.

Baby and toddler groups/playgroups: as Chloe, mother of Oliver and Elise, discovered: 'I found playgroups that had enough space for my toddler to run around in but which also had an area for babies (bouncy chairs, cushions) were great. It's good to be able not to have to hold your baby the whole time, so you can play with the toddler a little bit. There aren't that many places you can go to with two if you are breastfeeding and need to keep an eye on a toddler.' Baby and toddler groups are also a particularly good way of getting to meet other mums with children the same age as yours. This is invaluable if you've just moved to a new area and don't already have a network of friends. NCT coffee group meetings are brilliant too.

Friends' houses: What would we do without them? You get the adult company and your children get different toys to play with and a change of scene and it's cheaper than going to Starbucks.

Library: as you've probably already discovered with your first child, libraries are no longer just places for borrowing books. All sorts of activities seem to go on there and it's a wonderful centre for information about local events and what's going on where.

Story-time sessions are free and take place in larger libraries several times a week for babies and toddlers, and you can often take out up to ten books per child, which should keep you all going for a while.

Leisure centre: find out about all the activities your baby and toddler can take part in at your local leisure centre. Baby and toddler massage, yoga, bounceabout and baby swimming (though this can be a nightmare unless the changing rooms have the fold-down strap-on baby changing unit) are just some of the activities offered in my local leisure centre for this age group. There is also a crèche that takes babies from three months, which is helpful for when you need to concentrate on doing an activity with just one child, such as swimming (or, in fact, if you want to have a peaceful swim all by yourself). Joining too many classes will get expensive, but most places will let you attend a trial session to see whether you like it or not.

Cinema: this really depends on the temperament of your baby. The darkened room of the cinema was apparently the perfect environment for my baby to sleep so I could happily take him and my toddler to see an afternoon film. If the baby did wake up and want feeding, I could do this easily without anyone noticing or minding (which some people still do in some places).

Outdoor activities: a friend of mine used to play football with her football-mad five year old, with her baby strapped to her chest. Apparently the baby was quite happy, as was the five year old! On the whole, however, outdoor activities with two, while they are both little, are easiest done together as a family when they are more enjoyable. At weekends you can go and visit parks together and Dad can slide down the slide with the toddler while Mum sits on the swing with the baby, or go to museums or go on walks together. Cycling, with all the various add-on contraptions, is fun too. Doing things together as a family is a vital part of enjoying life with two children.

Different activities for girls and boys

While your children are young, they will probably be happy to try out most activities and do lots of the same things together. As they get older, you may find that your children want to do very different things, particularly if you have a boy and a girl. This is certainly what my sister-in-law has found with her son, Tom and daughter, Belle: 'The activities that they both enjoy are becoming rarer all the time and in spite of me using all my not inconsiderable powers of persuasion (think large bribes of the chocolate variety), Belle is not keen on soccer and Tom does not like dancing lessons. Things such as Beavers/Rainbows, ballet/soccer, yoga/rugby will inevitably be divided in terms of location and time, resulting in you spending even more of your life sitting in traffic or fruitlessly looking for parking places as you ferry your beloved male/female offspring to their respective clubs and activities. Swimming is a nice leveller, as is tennis: seriously consider these facts before you embrace very gender-specific hobbies. Belle hated having to watch almost three hours of cricket a week, which made the 180 minutes extremely tiresome and sadly 180 minutes during rush hour does not buy you many alternative activities when the cricket pitch is miles from anywhere.'

There is of course no guarantee that your two daughters or two sons will want to do the same things either, so just be prepared for working out how to juggle their different activities, and try and get to know as many of your children's friends' parents as you can, so you can organize sharing the driving of the children to and from their different classes.

Car journeys

Safety first

Making sure both your children are safe in the car is of course the number one priority, so do make sure you're up to date with the latest regulations regarding car seats and seat belts – the AA website is a good one to look at. Here are some things to be particularly aware of:

* Are your car seats fitted properly? According to research, two-thirds of car seats are fitted incorrectly and this means that your children won't be protected properly in the event of an accident. Take your car to your garage or local dealer and get them to check for you if you're not sure.
* You'll need to get your older child a toddler car seat and use the infant seat for your new baby.
* It's illegal to use rear-facing child seats in the front of your car if it is protected by a passenger-side airbag.

* Do your child restraints comply with UN ECE Regulation 44.03? They have to by law now.
* Check that your child locks are working in the back doors.
* Fit a rear-view mirror that allows you to see both your children without the need to turn around. By far the most car accidents with children in the car occur because the driver is distracted by their children in the back.

Tips for making car journeys easier with two

If you're going on a long car journey planning ahead will make things a lot easier:

* Do as much of a long trip as possible when your children are asleep. Wait until after the rush hour, pop your children into their night clothes and off you go. They'll probably quickly go to sleep so they won't get bored and you won't get distracted.
* If you've got to drive during the day, plan to stop roughly every couple of hours for loo breaks, refreshments, stretching legs and generally breaking up the monotony of the journey a bit. It's also better for the baby, according to health professionals, who warn that sitting in an upright position in a car seat for longer than two hours can be a health risk for babies who might have problems with restricted breathing. The advice is that babies should be taken out of their car seat and put down on a flat surface so they can kick their legs and stretch out.
* Your toddler will need things to do to keep them entertained so pack a bag with books, colouring things, a few toys, story tapes and snacks. For your baby, tie some toys to their car seat so they don't get lost or instantly dropped.

* As your children get older, you may find that car journeys get harder – being in a confined space for long periods of time is not conducive to peace and harmony between siblings. Give each child their own bag of things to keep them occupied rather than expecting them to share nicely.

If there are two adults in the car, you might want to split the seating arrangements so that the older child sits in the front, and an adult sits in the back with the younger one. There are no laws to prevent children from sitting in the front provided they are safely strapped in, although many people feel it is safer for children to sit in the back. Whether the non-driver sits in the front or the back, it's helpful if they can entertain the children with traditional car games for a while – I spy, Car colours (each child chooses a colour and then they spend the next five minutes – or however long – counting cars of their chosen colour, the one counting the most being the winner), who can be the first to spot a cow/sheep/plane, etc. This makes it easier for the driver to concentrate on driving and helps to keep the children happy. Of course the adults may have arguments about who drives and who entertains – take it in turns!

Going on holiday

The idea of a holiday is that you should come back feeling refreshed, relaxed and re-energized! But is this possible if you're going on holiday with a baby and toddler? Or are you bound to come home feeling even more stressed than before you left?

'You can do it,' says one friend, 'so long as you don't try and be too ambitious.' She described her first attempt at going on holiday abroad after her second daughter was born as being a disaster. She and her husband went to stay with friends in Greece with their four month old and eighteen month old – she vividly remembers the four-hour flight with screaming infants, then the ferry to the island with a buggy, backpack, portable cot, two infants and only two adults to carry all the suitcases, how all four shared a room and worried about waking the rest of the house while trying to be nice guests in the day – and how it left them feeling totally exhausted when they eventually returned to the UK. Her advice: 'Don't go abroad for two years after your second baby is born!'

Certainly many of the parents I spoke to found that staying in the UK for holidays with their children worked for them. It's cheaper (a major consideration once you've got two kids to pay for), feeding your children is easier (you know what the food is and where to get it), the unpredictability of the weather is predictable so you know what to pack and that it's unlikely your children will get sunstroke, and if everything goes horribly wrong, or if one of the children gets ill, you can get home quicker. We spent the first few years of our children's lives going to stay with family in Norfolk and we all have happy memories of these breaks away from home. British beaches may not quite measure up to the glamour of the Caribbean or even the Mediterranean, but at least the sand doesn't get so hot that your children can't play on it.

Children of all ages love the beach – it's the one place I can take all four of my children aged from three to fifteen and know that there is something to keep all of them happy. Once your baby can sit up unsupported they will love the feel of wriggling their toes in the sand and stuffing handfuls of it in their mouth, while your older toddler can spend hours building sandcastles, burying dad in the sand, searching for slimy seaweed, and paddling in the shallow pools. The best thing is that with young children who aren't yet tied into school holidays you can go on holiday at a time when the beach isn't too packed with crowds of other holiday-makers.

And if it rains? Go to the pier and let your children be mesmerized by the games arcade – or if that's too horrifying a thought, you can always find a nice National Trust house to visit, or a zoo or wild animal park. Perfect! Make the most of your children's malleability while you can (my older children now groan when I suggest going to visit an interesting country house).

Holidays abroad

Perhaps you feel, however, a holiday is really only a holiday if you have guaranteed sunshine. If you can afford it, there are now plenty of holiday travel companies catering for young families that will take all the stress out of holidaying abroad, even with two young children. Depending on how much time you want to spend with your children on holiday you can stay at hotels where baby and child-care sessions are run throughout the day, some for babies as young as ten weeks old. Organized children's suppers are provided with fun and games, and all the baby equipment you need can be pre-booked – from baby monitors, sterilizers, high chairs, baby baths to potties, etc., so you can travel relatively light (no struggling with travel cots and buggies as my friend in Greece had to do). Babysitting services are also provided so you can enjoy a child-free evening as well, happy in the knowledge that your children are safely cared for. A relaxing holiday indeed (though do be sure to pre-book all the child care you want before you go to ensure a place for your children).

Stress-free as these holidays undoubtedly are, they are also expensive. And some families may also prefer to holiday more independently. If you've confidently and successfully travelled abroad with your first child, you may want to continue to do so with your second child. But like doing anything with two children, don't expect it to be quite as easy, particularly the travelling there and back! Keeping two children happy on a flight is twice as much work.

Here are some tips on flying with two children:

Time: give yourself lots of it – far more than you think you'll need both for getting to the airport for check-in, and then for walking to the boarding gate. Trying to run with a toddler while holding the baby, to make it before the gates close, would not be a happy start to your holiday.

Queuing: bad enough on your own but queuing with two children is worse. If there's a long queue to check in and you're travelling with another adult, get one person to look after the children while the other one queues and text them when you're getting near to the front.

Seats: comfortable seating arrangements are key to a more restful flight. You won't need to pay for a seat for your baby, but check what the airline can offer in terms of sky-cots and bassinets. They should be available for babies aged up to twelve months (or 11 kilograms/24 pounds in weight) and if you're on a long-haul flight, being able to lie your baby down to sleep will be a huge help. If your toddler is under two, they are eligible to fly free if they sit on your lap, but having a baby and/or a toddler on your lap for the whole flight will be very uncomfortable (please note use of understatement here). So if you can afford it book a seat for your toddler. Sit with the baby at an aisle seat if you can, so you can easily get up and walk your baby up and down if you need to. When your children are older, don't reserve seats so that you all sit together in a row. Both children will want to sit by a window, so if you can try and get two window seats directly in front of or behind each other, splitting one parent per child, that is the best arrangement. On your own with two children, they'll have to take it in turns to sit by the window.

Meals: whatever you may think of airline food, the meals do at least give you and your children something to do! But it's also quite nice if your children can eat the food too, so it's worth ordering special meals before you fly. You can then ensure your children get a meal they actually like. If you order everyone a separate meal you can mix and match, and hopefully there'll be something that everyone will want to eat. Ask the flight attendant to serve your children first and you last – after the other passengers. This will allow you to help your children eat their meal (take wrappers and lids off, etc.), without trying to balance your own meal on your tray. Once your children are eating, you may be able to eat your own meal in relative peace. If you are flying on a budget airline that doesn't offer complimentary meals, take a picnic that includes lots of easy finger foods for your children to munch on, rather than buying the often overpriced on-board meals.

Avoid spending too much time in aeroplane loos: no one likes tiny aeroplane loos, or queuing for them, so the less time you can spend in there with your children the better. Take your toddler to the loo before you board the plane and change your baby's nappy too – put on a super-absorbent one, and if you normally use re-usable cloth nappies, consider disposables for the holiday. Don't let your child drink sugary drinks that will make them need the loo more. This also means you don't have to feel guilty for not taking them to the loo to brush their teeth.

In-flight entertainment: with a toddler and small baby, that's probably you. But do bring each a separate bag of things for them to do – and maybe even a surprise new toy for your toddler to unwrap on the plane. To avoid hatred-filled stares from other passengers, don't pack your toddler's favourite electronic noisy fire-engine, or your baby's bell rattle, and pack soft toys not hard plastic ones so if any get thrown and hit a neighbour, at least it won't hurt so much.

Finally, good luck and have a great holiday.

Time out for yourself

Time. You just don't seem to have any with two children to look after. As my sister-in-law put it so succinctly: 'If you haven't already done so, cancel one of the following: social life/extended family life/working life/gym membership. Accept it, your life is going to change (again) and you are going to wonder what you did with all that free time you had BC2 (before child 2).' You may have thought you were busy enough with one child, but wait until you have two!

When you have one child it is easier for you and your partner to take it in turns to do the child care while the other one has a bit of time to themselves. When you have two children this becomes much harder, particularly as your children get a bit older and need to be in two different places at the same time. One parent takes one child, the other parent takes the other – time on your own is hard to come by.

But while I agree with my sister-in-law that having two children does of course mean you have even less time for yourself – there are some days when you don't even seem to have time to go to the loo on your own – this doesn't mean you should give up on the idea of having any time for yourself. Your children mean everything to you, but you are important too. You need to have some time out for yourself, away from your children just to keep sane, to keep on going in fact. And don't feel guilty about it. If you start to feel guilty (as I used to the minute I did something for myself without my children) remember that:

* having a break from your children helps you to enjoy your time more when you are with them
* your children will benefit from spending some time with other people
* it's in everyone's interests if you don't have a nervous breakdown.

You are not being self-indulgent; you are preserving yourself so you can continue to be a good mother. Do whatever you enjoy doing – see friends, go to a movie, do spinning classes at the gym, have a long and luxurious bubble bath and read a book, get your hair done – enough to stop feeling swamped by all your responsibilities. Get your partner to look after the children (you can return the favour so he can go out and do his own thing too) – or, if that's not possible, find a babysitter – just make sure you do, both, have some time for yourselves.

Time out with your partner

Mums on time out with your partner:
'We have much less time to spend with each other but we both know that it's only short term and that in a few years, we'll have more time for each other. It's the price you pay for having children!'

Chloe, mother of Oliver and Elise

'Having two children so close together (there are only 13 months between them) definitely affects your relationship. There is no time really for you and your partner. Your babies are too young to be left with anyone they don't know well, and not many people want to take that on.'

Clare, mother of Isabelle, Grace and Sam

A few years ago I remember watching a TV show that showed parents how to resolve their children's sleep problems. One particular couple had a toddler who stayed up with them every night until he eventually fell asleep at about 11 o'clock. The couple never had an evening to themselves. They followed the advice of the sleep expert, which was very good, and within less than a week the toddler was going to bed at a reasonable time and the parents had their evenings back to themselves again. A great success. Except that within a month the parents separated – they realized they had nothing to say to each other. With two children, you are both so busy that it is easy to become like ships that pass in the night, hardly ever seeing each other, no time for conversations that consist of anything more than 'Have you seen the baby wipes?' or 'What time are you coming home tonight?' so it is perhaps not surprising that some studies suggest that the most difficult time for a marriage is not after your first child is born, but after your second. Money is tighter, sleep is scarcer, responsibilities are greater, stress is higher and your sex life may be temporarily non-existent.

It is even more difficult for couples who were having problems before their second baby. For those who think that having a second child may help to stick together a bad relationship, the advice is to think again. Evidence suggests that where there are already problems in a marriage, a second child makes things worse. Mothers can easily feel resentful that their partner doesn't help enough, and feel angry that they have to do so much work with little support even when their partner is at home. Dads can feel that they have to work long and hard at the office and need some rest at home to be able to function properly in the office. Stereotypical, but typical for many nonetheless. The argument about who does the most work and who is the most exhausted is a very common one – studies show that when asked about particular chores like doing the laundry, cooking meals, housework, doing repairs in the house, etc., each person thinks they contribute more than the other. In addition, there may be arguments about how to raise two children: different approaches to child-rearing and discipline become apparent and can cause tensions.

For any relationship to survive, you need to work at it, and taking time out to be with your partner is one of the most important ways of doing this. If you make the time to be on your own together and to communicate with each other, small irritations and problems are less likely to become big ones and end up in arguments and fights. You may think your partner should understand how you are feeling but unless you talk about your feelings, and make the time to tell each other how you feel, he probably won't know and you won't be able to resolve the problems. If you and your partner are happy together and have a good relationship, the likelihood is that your children will be happier too. Taking the time to do things together is important for the happiness of the whole family.

Your sex life

When you're up all night feeding a baby, and on your feet all day looking after both your children, the idea of being energetic in bed with your husband is probably the last thing on your mind. While you are concentrating so hard on being a perfect mother to your two children, being a perfect wife often comes lower down on your list of priorities. Sex can feel like just another chore that at the end of the day you are too exhausted to contemplate – all you really want to do in bed is go to sleep. Most women need to wait between a month and six weeks before feeling physically ready for sex again. After a second baby it may take longer before being emotionally ready for it. But ignoring your sex life for too long can become a problem – a good sex life is often an important part of a good relationship. To begin with, just spending some time alone together, being loving to each other, even if it is only to hug each other can ease tensions and make you happier as a couple, rather than simply being parents to your children.

How to find the time for each other

Unless you plan this, the reality is it probably won't happen. You'll both be too tired and end up falling asleep without so much as a good-night kiss. The way many couples find time for each other is to plan a regular date – every week, fortnight or month – where they go out and spend time together, going out to dinner or doing something they both enjoy together. This is how Gayle, mother of Theo and twins Katia and Adelaide managed: 'We had a sixteen-year-old neighbour who came in after school on a Friday, played with our son, bathed and fed the three of them, read them stories, tidied away their toys and put them all to bed. I meanwhile put on some clean, non-child messed clothes, took a healthy walk into town, met my husband for a glass of wine and some tapas and was home by 8pm, a refreshed, rejuvenated woman, with a healthy relationship with my husband, ready to tackle the weekend with everyone demanding a piece of me.'

Babysitters can be expensive but if you trade with friends so you babysit for each other, it makes it easier. Getting out of the house and away from your everyday routine environment helps you relax, and makes it easier to focus on each other rather than the mound of ironing or washing-up. But you don't always have to go out to spend time alone together. Order an occasional take-away meal and eat together when the children have gone to sleep, or watch a movie together on TV – although it's important to find time to talk to each other, sometimes just spending quiet, undemanding time together can be what you need, so long as you're not using the TV as an excuse not to talk to each other. Even spending fifteen minutes together at the end of the day helps you to stay connected and to remember your importance to each other. But don't spend it talking about the children – however hard it is to think of another topic of conversation to begin with.

Having two children can make your relationship stronger

While the stresses of looking after two children are exhausting and can put a strain on your marriage, they can also make your relationship stronger. A good marriage can become a great one if you can help each other cope with the trials and tribulations of raising two children together. Often it is only after the birth of a second child that the father becomes really involved in family life and it becomes clearer that his role is not just to go out and earn money, as many men may feel after one child. Helping more with the care of the children – whether it's developing a stronger relationship with your first-born while you take more care of the baby, or soothing the baby while you play with your toddler – can make you feel a greater sense of partnership. And of course having two children is a great joy too. The shared love that you have for them both can increase the love and respect you have for each other, and give you a deeper and even more solid commitment to your relationship.

EIGHT

Money matters and going back to work

Raising just one child to the age of eighteen can cost a small fortune so how on earth is one supposed to be able to afford to bring up two? It's no wonder that many parents think long and hard about their financial situation and spend a great deal of time planning, budgeting and saving before committing themselves to the expense of having a second child. You've probably already made some financial sacrifices to have your first child – and you'll have to make even more to have another. And yet, the majority of parents do go on to have a second child – not just parents with huge bank accounts, but couples from all sorts of economic backgrounds – some in work and some not. As one mother of two said to me, 'You do just manage somehow. You've already got lots of things you can reuse from your first child, and people give you lots of things too. So long as you can keep your children warm and fed and loved, they don't need to have expensive stuff. You might know the difference between Armani and Asda but your children don't.' Perhaps it's just better not to know how much it's meant to cost to bring up two children. As many parents have said to me, 'If you wait until you can afford a second baby, you'll never have one.'

The good news is that having a second child does not cost as much as having your first one. In fact, studies show that a second child costs only about half as much as a first to raise to age eighteen. Less than 15 per cent of family income is typically spent on a second child compared with 30 per cent for a first. For a start, unless your children are born very close together, you won't have to fork out for some of the most expensive equipment, like another cot, high chair, baby car seat, sling and feeding equipment; baby clothes and toys can all be reused too. Additionally, being a more experienced parent means you are able to make better decisions about what you actually need to buy. Many of the gadgets you are led to believe are essential for your first baby, you learn you can live without and don't need for your second.

Nevertheless, while it may not cost much more to have a second child in the short term, it's pointless to pretend that it won't cost a great deal more in the longer term. The increased cost of child care if you and your partner both decide to go back to work, or the continued loss of income if one of you decides to stay at home, is the biggest expenditure; then there's the cost of education – with uniform, school trips and equipment and university fees later on; the cost of holidays – especially once your children are at school and you have to take them in the school holidays; the cost of outings and activities, and food all add up to a frightening amount. Ignoring these difficult money facts, and deciding to 'cross that bridge when you come to it', I happen to know from experience doesn't mean the financial problems go away. Quite the reverse, in fact. Doing what you can to plan ahead for these costs, and keeping your finances under control, are an essential part of surviving life with two children. You'll have quite enough sleepless nights already without adding more by worrying how you'll get through to the end of the month.

Here are some ways to make bringing up two children more affordable.

Claim your grants and benefits from the government

You can still claim benefits from the government to help with the costs of looking after your children, and it's absolutely worth making sure you know what there is and what you're entitled to. It can make a very real difference, but if you don't claim you won't get. Here's a list of some of the most important ones. If you're already claiming on the basis of one child, you'll need to let them know about your second.

Child benefit: once you've registered your baby, you'll be able to claim child benefit for your second child. Don't forget that you need to fill in a form and apply for it. The amount is slightly lower than for your first child but it can be a very useful sum. If you can afford to and haven't done this already, arrange for this to be paid into a separate child account and don't touch it until you need to buy something big for your children (computer, school trip, etc.). If it goes straight into your current account, it will be swallowed up and disappear along with everything else.

Maternity benefits

Statutory maternity pay: if you went back to work after your first baby, have been with your company for at least twenty-six weeks at the fifteenth week before the week of your due date and earn an average of at least £90 a week before tax, you'll qualify for statutory maternity pay again. This is currently 90 per cent of your average weekly earnings for the first six weeks of maternity leave and then a standard rate for the remaining thirty-three weeks. You are paid for a total of thirty-nine weeks – the remaining thirteen weeks that you are allowed to take off work will be unpaid. Note that because maternity pay is not a benefit

197

but a replacement for your income, it is taxed in the same way as your normal pay.

SureStart maternity grant: this is a one-off payment to help towards the cost of a new baby if you're on a low income. The grant comes from the Social Fund and you don't have to repay it and it doesn't affect other benefits.

Maternity allowance: if you are self-employed or haven't been employed long enough to qualify for statutory maternity pay, you are eligible for a maternity allowance. This is currently a standard sum of £124.88 or 90 per cent of your average gross weekly earnings, whichever is the smaller.

Getting help with the cost of child care – tax credits and child-care vouchers

For many parents the decision about whether to go back to work after a second child is a financial one (see page 203 for more about going back to work). The cost of child care for two children is the biggest expense you face. Because the government is keen to encourage people back to work, there are working tax credits and child-care vouchers to make it easier. It can be confusing, though, to work out which will be of greater benefit.

* **Working tax credits** can be claimed if you are working more than sixteen hours a week – the amount will depend on your income. Additionally, if you are eligible for the child-care element, the tax credits will pay the equivalent of 80 per cent of child-care costs provided by a registered child-minder, out-of-school club or another approved provider. To find out exactly what you would receive, talk to an experienced adviser at your local Citizens Advice Bureau.

* **Child-care vouchers** are operated through employers and they allow you to pay for your child care from your salary before tax, which can save you thousands of pounds. If both parents are working, you are each allowed a maximum amount per month worth of vouchers. However, if you are eligible for child care tax credits, the vouchers can limit the amount of tax credits you get and you may be worse off if you take them, so check first. If your company doesn't provide the vouchers it's worth persuading them to do so as it doesn't cost them any more – in fact, as they don't pay National Insurance on the vouchers, they should save money by providing them.

Save for your child's future

Child trust fund (CTF)

If your first child was born after 1 September 2002, you will have already received a voucher from the government to start up a tax-free savings and investment account for them – currently worth £250. For newborns born between 1 August and 31 December 2010, you will get a voucher too, but the amount has been cut to £50 (or £100 for low-income families). After this date the government plan to abolish the trust funds altogether, although the account set up for your first child will continue to be eligible for tax-free savings until he or she reaches eighteen, when they will have full control of the money – a considerable sum, which may help with the cost of their university fees. If your second child does not qualify for the benefit of a trust fund from the government, if at all possible, do try and set up a similar savings account for them yourself. There are several tax-free saving schemes to choose from, including children's bonus bonds, index-linked savings certificates and premium bonds. Have a look on the internet or speak to an independent financial adviser for the best deals around.

Save money

There are all sorts of ways to save money without necessarily having to give up everything that makes life enjoyable, and without denying your children either. Here are some tips:

Recycle and reuse everything: for your second child, you will be able to reuse a great deal of the stuff you bought for your first child, especially if you bought neutral-coloured clothes. Not that it really matters if your baby boy wears his older sister's pink babygro, but later on he may mind. Keep everything you bought for your first child and if your second child doesn't need it, give it to someone who does. A quick note of caution here, though. Second children get used to wearing their big brother or sister's cast-offs, but can resent it if they never get anything new. Make sure you do sometimes buy your second child something new, specifically for them, and that it's not always your first child who has new things.

Use washable cloth nappies: you'll make the greatest saving if you used them for your first child, but even if you didn't it's still worth buying them for your second. Not only will you save money, but you'll be doing your bit to save the environment too. And if the idea of all that extra washing puts you off, look into the laundry services that will do all this for you. Some local councils provide a nappy collection service for free so it won't cost you more to do this.

Buy secondhand: when children grow out of their clothes so quickly, there is little point in spending a lot of money on something they will only be able to wear for a few months – even if you are passing it down to your second child. The same is true of toys, too. Children apparently break 40 per cent of the toys they are given within the first three months, so again it makes much more sense to buy toys secondhand. Go to jumble sales, car boot sales, nearly new sales and charity shops – you can pick up some great bargains and save yourself a lot of money. (Shoes are the only things I would buy new as it's important to make sure they fit properly.)

Buy and sell online: you can make a surprising amount of money by selling any unwanted or outgrown toys and clothes on internet auction sites like eBay. If you haven't done this before it is very easy to set up – get a knowledgeable friend to come over and show you how, and then raid your children's cupboards for things they no longer need. Just make sure you have included the cost of posting the items or you may find yourself out of pocket. eBay is a good place to look for cheap items to buy too – both new and secondhand – though, again, check the postage costs to make sure you really are saving money.

Friends can save you money: by the time your second child comes along you will probably have quite a few friends with children and this network is incredibly important for all sorts of reasons – including saving you money:

* Share baby equipment and lend each other things your children have outgrown or aren't playing with – it helps if your children are slightly different ages so they don't need the same things at the same time.

* Club together and buy things in bulk at a discount price and share the items out between you.

* Lift-share and cut the cost of driving – this is particularly helpful in country areas where public transport is not so frequent or available.

* Babysit for each other and make going out in the evening more affordable.

* Nanny share: hiring a nanny to look after your children is expensive but if you share the cost with a friend, it becomes much easier.
* And, of course, visiting each other's houses, instead of paying to take your child to soft play – again – saves you money too.

Save money on holidays: if you've been used to spending an annual holiday abroad, you can save a great deal of money by staying in Britain for your holiday, or staying at home and going for days out. But if you do want to go abroad on holiday, go before your children start school – you can save an average of 37 per cent by being able to go on holiday at non-peak times outside the school holidays. Additionally, planning for your holiday and booking it as far ahead as possible will save you money too – flights are much cheaper if you can book up to a year in advance. Having said that, at the moment you can get some very good deals if you are prepared to leave it until the last minute – if you become desperate to get away, it's worth checking your travel agent for their late deals.

Cut food bills: breastfeeding is obviously the cheapest way to feed your baby, but it isn't long before you will need to buy solid food for two children. The more children you have the greater the savings you'll make by cooking your own food rather than buying baby food or ready prepared meals. It's worth cooking in bulk and freezing what you don't need in portion sizes – it will save you time too. Doing your supermarket shop online saves a lot of money – it's much easier to compare prices and make sure you are getting the best deal, and it's much easier to stick to your budget and buy only what you need. Buying food from your local market if you have one is often cheaper than buying from the shops. If you or your partner can, go at the end of the day when they're selling things off cheap to get rid of them, and you'll get some great bargains.

Going back to work

The decision about whether to go back to work becomes much more difficult after your second child is born. While around 80 per cent of mothers return to work of some type after their first child, this number decreases significantly after a second child for a whole number of different reasons. For some mothers, like Nicola, having a second child gave her the excuse she needed to give up work for a bit. 'I'd always planned to go back to work after my first child was born and I didn't really think about it, although it was harder than I imagined. But after Sam was born it was different. The pull to stay at home was much greater. Somehow it seemed worse to leave two children to be looked after by someone else and I just didn't think I could do it. With two children to look after I felt I had more of a justification for staying at home and not going back to work. Also, by this time, my husband was earning more so it was easier for us to afford it if I didn't work for a few years.'

For Clare, knowing that her second child would be her last child, made her decide to take time off work. 'I went back to work six months after Jack, my first child, was born and I felt I was missing out on so much. When Joe was born I didn't want to miss seeing all those firsts again – his first steps, his first words – and worrying that somebody else would see them instead of me. This was my last chance to see my children growing up and I didn't want to miss it.' Other mothers decide that the stress of trying to combine working full time with looking after two children is simply too much, and that waiting until their children go to school is the best option for them. Other women will decide to continue working but to decrease the number of hours they work, while in other families the dad decides to stay at home. There are a great many different ways of living, working and enjoying your children and just as many different reasons behind the choices you make.

To go back to work or not?

Can you afford it? For many couples, financial considerations are the overriding factor in whether to return to work, although perhaps in ways you might not expect. Women who are highly paid and highly skilled, who might more easily be able to afford to stay at home, are in fact more likely to return to work after both children because the rewards are greater. Women on the lowest incomes are least likely to go back to work. For many other women, going back to work only just covers the cost of child care for two and very little else, but the prospect of being able to earn more with promotion makes a return to work necessary in the long term.

What about your career? If you're ambitious and on a career ladder, you may be worried about taking time out to look after the children. How easy will it be to get back into work after taking a break, and will you get a job at the same level and position and salary? The longer you leave it, the harder it seems to become.

Do you enjoy staying at home with your children? You or your partner may love being at home with your children and find the idea of being parted from them to go back to work unbearable. In this case, however difficult the financial situation, the decision can be much easier to make. But many parents are more torn. They love their children and do not want to miss out on watching them growing up, but at the same time they do not want to stay at home to be with them all day, every day. If you find it easier to go to work and have some time away from your children, so you can enjoy them more when you are with them, for some people this may be the answer. It can be very lonely and isolating looking after children – perhaps it's not surprising that women who stay at home are more likely to suffer from depression than women who go back to work – and of course it's hard work.

It's not just the actual care of your children but all the work that goes with it – the cleaning, tidying, cooking, washing and so on. Not everyone is suited to this; and knowing yourself – knowing what you are good at and what you can cope with – is an important part of making a decision about whether or not to go back to work.

Different ways of working

● *Working full time*

If you and your partner both went back to work after your first child, you'll already know that juggling work and home life takes a huge amount of time, requires a lot of organization and can be exhausting. Trying to do this for two children is even more so. If your children are going to be looked after somewhere else outside your home, you have to get them up in the morning, dressed, clean and fed, remember to pack everything that two children need for the day, then get them into the car or buggy to get to their day care before getting yourself to work on time making sure that you've remembered everything you need for work and that you haven't got a sticky jam smudge on your shirt. At the end of the working day, crossing your fingers that you aren't stuck in a meeting or traffic, you have two children to collect, to take home and play with, bath, read stories to, put to bed and you still haven't finished. After your children are asleep is when you start all the household jobs. And even when you've finished those and you fall into bed, you may be woken in the night by a sick or unsettled child.

According to various statistics, women with young children who work full time:

* sleep less (forty minutes less a night) and work more than any other women

* do about two-and-a-half hours 'domestic work' every day
* have a total of seven hours 'me' time per week – compared to almost seventeen hours for women without children who work.

It sounds exhausting and it is. 'I don't go to bed, I pass out with tiredness every night, and I still don't feel as though I've got everything done that I need to,' said one working mother of two to me who returned to work full time three months ago. 'But it's getting a little better now that we've all more-or-less got used to the routines. I'm getting better at making lists and remembering what I'm supposed to be doing every day.'

While it is very tiring, many women find that going back to work full time is very rewarding, as Gina, a designer for a publishing firm, told me: 'I love my work and I think I'm a better mum because I work full time. I know my children are happy at their day care nursery. They go there three days a week; my partner does shift work so he looks after them one day a week; and my mum looks after them at home the other day. I think we've got the balance right. It's good for the children to play with other children their own age at nursery, but they've still got some time at home and they're very close to their dad and their granny. At weekends, we've got a bit more money in our pockets to do things so we can enjoy life.'

● *How to survive the juggling act*
Organization: you have to become good at this to survive. Write lists for the week ahead – meals, shopping, work commitments, any social engagements, and work out what needs to be done for everyone on each day of the week. Get everything ready for each day the night before – what you'll wear, your children's clothes, their bags – and yours.

Make the most of your time with your children: it can be particularly hard for your firstborn child when you go back to work for a second time. They have enjoyed spending more time with you while you've been at home, but when you go back to work they not only see you less during the day but also have to share you with their sibling when you get home from work:

* You may not have much time with them during the week, but try and make sure that the time you do have is happy – leave the housework and chores until after they've gone to bed and play with your children while you can. Try not to bring work home with you so that you can give your children undivided attention when you are with them.

* Some parents try and keep their children up late so they get a bit more time with them after work. This is fine, provided that your children are getting enough overall sleep during the day – either with longer daytime naps, or if they can sleep for longer in the mornings. If they can't make up the extra time, it's better for them to sleep at their earlier bedtime, and for you to make the most of your time with them at weekends.

* Make sure you have a good relationship with your children's carer and have time to talk to them at the end of each day to find out what your children have been doing and how they are.

Divide the work load with your partner: life is a lot easier if you can share the work involved in looking after your children and household chores equally with your partner. If you haven't done this already, work out a rota of who will collect the children on which days or drop them off in the morning, and agree how to split up the work that needs doing in the house.

Support network: having back-up support – whether from family or friends – who can help you out if one or other of your children are ill, or if you and your partner are both going to be held up at work, makes life a lot less stressful. Keep a list of people you can ring in emergencies stored in your mobile phone.

Babysitters: you need to have a bit of fun and relaxation time. Whenever you can, hire a babysitter so you can go out, if only for a couple of hours, and spend time with your partner and friends. If you can find a babysitter who will also do some ironing at the same time, that's even better.

Avoiding stress: work out the things that make you feel most stressed and make a plan. There are usually certain times in the day you find most stressful, or particular things that you find hard. It might be first thing in the morning when you're trying to get everyone out of the house, it might be mealtimes when you're trying to get your elder child to eat his peas and your second child to eat anything at all, or bedtime when your patience is at its lowest ebb and your children refuse to go to sleep. Maybe it's certain days of the week that are particularly stressful because of all the things you are meant to do on that day, or it's the household things. Look objectively at these most stressful moments – when you're not feeling stressed – and see if you can simplify things, or find solutions. It might be getting up ten minutes earlier in the morning so you have more time perhaps, or start your children's bedtime earlier. Shift an activity to a different day. There may be many things you can do to make life a bit easier if you take the time to have a look at it. And find ways of helping yourself to feel less stressed. Maybe taking up yoga will help, or learning some other relaxation techniques.

Remember, the first day back is the worst. Saying goodbye to your children and leaving them with someone else is really hard, but it does get easier – for all of you. In some ways it can be easier saying goodbye in the morning to two children because you know they've got each other. But if after a few months you are still finding things hard and that working full time is not paying dividends for you or your children, you can reconsider your options. Perhaps there is another way of working that will suit you all better.

Tips for overcoming tiredness in the office

* Don't visit that coffee machine too many times and don't drink any coffee after lunch – you won't get to sleep at night, so you'll be even more tired the next day. Drink as much water as you can instead.

* In your lunch hour, go outside for a walk – fresh air will wake you up.

* Or, if you can, take a short, fifteen-minute 'power nap'. They can be amazingly energizing.

● *Flexi-time and part-time work*

After a second child many parents decide they want to change the way they work. Provided you've been with your company for at least twenty-six weeks (including the period on maternity leave) you are legally entitled to ask your employer for a change in your work pattern. Your employer must seriously consider your request and have a good business reason for refusing. There are various different ways you can ask to work more flexibly.

Recent studies have shown that most mothers want to be able to work part time – it seems to promise the perfect balance of spending time with your children at home while also having time in an adult work environment and the rewards – both financial and intellectual

– of working. But before asking your employer if you can drop the number of hours or days you work a week, it's worth considering how you think your job can be done in less time. Are there parts of the job that can be done by other people, or will you end up doing the same amount of work but just in less time and for less money? Some jobs are not easily done on a part-time basis and you may find that you will need to apply for a different job if you want to work fewer hours.

I have spoken to women who felt that working part time was the worst of both worlds; not having enough time to do either their job or look after their children properly. It's worth pointing out, too, that some people find they are taken less seriously and their commitment to the job is questioned if they ask to reduce their hours. On the other hand, if you have a good relationship with your employer, your going part time may work very well for them if it means that you continue to work for them rather than leave altogether. When your children are older you may then up your hours again to working full time. If you are the boss in your department, or of your company, you may have a better understanding of how easy (or not) it will be to change your pattern of working. Having a good second in command, and being able to delegate work will be the key issues here.

Other ways of working more flexibly, enabling you to spend more time with your children, include working flexi-time – doing the same number of hours but at different times to fit in with your children – i.e. starting earlier or later so that you can finish earlier or later and have time with your children in the mornings or evenings. Perhaps working compressed hours would suit you, so instead of working for thirty-five hours a week over five days, you fit the same number of hours into four days. You should then be able to retain your current salary level while making more time for your children at home and reducing the cost of child care.

When presenting any of these proposals to change your working patterns to your boss, do as much homework and preparation beforehand as you can. If you can, speak to other colleagues who have done the same thing, find out what the advantages and disadvantages are for you and your employer, and come up with as many solutions to the problems as you can.

● *Working from home*

There are lots of advantages to being able to work from home if the sort of work you do allows it – and with the sort of IT now available an increasing number of jobs can be done from home. Having a commute that takes all of thirty seconds instead of an hour-and-a-half or more every day, gives you much more time to spend with your children (and to work) and is much cheaper, the flexibility of being at home meaning you can arrange to do things in your own time and that it is easier for you to manage full-time work as well as your home life.

For many parents it's the ideal way of working and, as I myself work from home, I can say from experience that the benefits are many. I can also say that there are some pitfalls too. If your children are being looked after in your home (and you will still need child care despite what you may think) it is hard for them to understand why you're unavailable and can't play with them if you're at home. It's hard for you, too, to hear your children and not be distracted by them or want to go to them. If you take your children to be looked after somewhere else, you've still got to ignore your domestic surroundings (the pile of washing up in the sink, the laundry that needs doing, etc.) and stay focused on your work. Working from home can be quite lonely too – you don't have the social interaction of the office, nor do you have the benefit of being in a different environment, other than the study instead of the kitchen.

Getting the right child care

Every working parent knows that you can only be happy at work if your children are being cared for well. Finding the right child care for your children is essential for them and for you. But what worked well when you had one child, may not work so well when you have two children, whose needs and requirements are different, and you may find that you need to look at your child-care options again.

Keep it in the family

If you're lucky enough to have grandparents living nearby you may be among the 50 per cent of working parents who rely on them for child care. If so, you'll already be aware of all the benefits of having close family look after your child – the strong family bonds that are made, the flexibility and continuity of care – not to mention the cost. Many grandparents provide child care for free or at a fraction of the cost of ordinary child care. (You may also be aware of the problems of family providing child care – if you have different opinions about behaviour and discipline for example.) But asking grandparents to take on the care of a second child as well is a big ask. Is it fair to them, and is it fair for your children? If you found it exhausting looking after two children, it will be no less so for the grandparents who will be older and may find it physically more demanding. Perhaps they were looking forward to having a bit of a break and doing some things for themselves when your first child was old enough to attend nursery. Think back to their reaction when you told them the news you were pregnant again! You will need to have a thorough discussion with the grandparents to see what they might be happy to take on. Perhaps they would find it easier to look after the new baby, while your older child goes to nursery, or they might be happy to look after both children but for fewer days a week or fewer hours in a day. Sit down with them, talk about all the options and be prepared to find some alternative care if necessary.

Nanny/nanny share

A qualified nanny who comes to look after your children in your own home so you don't need to worry about getting your children ready before you go to work, who can cook for your children, do their laundry, tidy their rooms and take them to their activities can seem ideal. The trouble is that this can be an expensive option, particularly if you are solely responsible for paying their salary. Often the solution is to do a nanny share with another family so you split the costs. If nanny sharing with your friends isn't an option, there are websites that will help you find families in your area who are looking to share a nanny. This is what we did. When I went back to work after my first child was born, we employed a professionally trained nanny who we shared with another family who had school-age children. Harry was looked after on his own in our home until it was time to collect the other two children from school when they all went back to their home. It worked perfectly, and sharing the cost made it affordable, until we had our second child and moved house. We then employed a nanny who had a child of her own whom she brought to work with her and the nanny looked after all the children in our house. She only stopped working for us after her second child was born, but our children have grown up together as friends, her support made it possible for me to continue working happily and she is now godmother to our fourth child!

It may be more difficult to share a nanny with another family after your second child is born, depending on how many children you both have and whether you need the nanny to look after all your children together. However, you may find that there is not that much difference in cost between being the sole employer to your nanny and paying for a daycare nursery for two children, particularly if your nanny is registered and you can claim tax credits or use your child-care vouchers. It may take a couple of months to get all the documents and process them for a nanny to become registered if they have not done so already but it is worth doing from both your points of view. Consider contributing to the cost of your nanny getting herself registered – Ofsted charges £135 a year and the first aid certificate that is required costs £150.

Registered child-minder

A good registered child-minder who looks after children in her own home may be much more affordable than either a nanny or a daycare nursery, and if your first child is already being looked after by one you may not want to change this arrangement. Child-minders provide a homely, safe environment, they can often be more flexible about hours as they are working in their own home and as they look after other children as well, it can be fun for your child to be able to socialize and have different opportunities for play. But the question is whether your child-minder is able to accommodate your new baby. Child-minders are only allowed to look after three children under the age of five, and usually only one baby under twelve months. If your child-minder is full up, what do you do? It may just be a question of waiting a few months until an older child leaves to go to school or no longer needs child care, but if the wait is any longer you will need to think whether you find alternative temporary child care just for your baby or whether you move your first child and find somewhere new where both children can be looked after together.

Nursery/daycare

There are many advantages to daycare nurseries, as you will know if you have used one for your first child. They are open all year round, they have lots of trained staff so you never have to worry about your child-minder being off sick, they have a wide variety of toys, activities and equipment, there are other children to play with, and there is usually a programme of learning to help your child's development at whatever stage they're at. There are disadvantages, too, of course. You can't send a child to nursery if they've got a temperature or are sick; and the chances of one or both your children picking something up at nursery are fairly high given the number of children they are mixing with. There is little flexibility over the hours (though many are open from 7am to 7pm) and tough penalties if you're late. Daycare nurseries have separate baby units to care for babies from the age of three or four months, so they should easily be able to accommodate the care of both of your children, but you need to consider whether you are happy for your baby – as well as your older child – to spend so many hours a day in a non-home environment. The cost of sending two children to daycare nursery will probably double too – though sibling discounts of around 5 per cent are often offered. Again, your tax credits or child-care vouchers can help with the cost of the nursery.

Dads and child care

While some mothers have told me that their partners coped with a second child by spending even more time at work, and while apparently only 10 per cent of dads take the full two weeks of paternity leave they are entitled to, many fathers are becoming much more involved in their children's care. With more flexible employment patterns, the options of working from home or changing their hours, working dads find it easier to take care of their children too, and the notion that child care is primarily the mother's responsibility is beginning to lessen – though gradually. Couples no longer automatically assume that it will be the mother who stops work and stays at home. 'We felt it was important for our children to be looked after by one of their parents,' Richard told me, father of Milly and Tom, 'and it made sense for it to be me. We were on roughly the same salary but as an architect it was easier for me to do some work from home as well as look after the children. I'll build up the business when Tom starts nursery in a year's time.' According to statistics, if you are a dad who is staying at home to look after the children you are one of about 200,000 other dads in the UK who are doing the same thing, either because their partners earn more money and it makes more sense for the dad to stay at home, or they are a single dad or because the dad actively chooses to stay at home. There is no doubt that society is changing and that the great benefits to children of fathers being more involved in their children's care are being recognized. This does not mean it is easy for dads – the chances are you won't see that many other dads pushing the double buggy to drop their toddler off for a session at nursery (at my son's nursery I only see a couple of dads a few times a week who come to pick up their children), or traipsing around the supermarket during the week with a baby in the sling and a small child in the trolley seat. But it's getting easier – there are even some playgroups run by dads for dads with their children. Look around for what's available on the internet, in your doctor's surgery and the local paper. Having friends to talk to and do things with while you're looking after children makes it easier and more fun.

Guilt and going back to work

Guilt and being a parent go together. It doesn't matter what the subject is, there's usually something to feel guilty about, and guilt about going back to work – or not – comes pretty high up on the list. Some parents feel guilty about leaving their children in order to work – feel even worse if they secretly enjoy being without their children for a little bit – and they feel guilty for putting themselves and their career before their children. Equally, other parents feel guilty for staying at home and denying their children opportunities because there's less money to go around, or for conforming to a traditional stereotype and not demon-strating to their children that they can be *anything* when they grow up. Either way, you can feel pretty awful. All I can say is, don't! Guilt is only a worthwhile emotion if it can produce something good. Instead of feeling guilty, try and get things into perspective. You know you love your children and that you will do as much as you can for them to make them happy. But for a family to work well, it needs to be balanced and for everyone's needs to be taken into consideration. If you are happy and successful – whether that's by staying at home or going out to work – you will be more able to keep your children happy. It's worth remem-bering that research shows there is no difference academically or socially between children who come from homes where both parents work or from a home where one parent stays at home.

Conclusion – how to stay sane

Looking after two children is full of contradictions – it's wonderful and it's wretched, it's exciting and it's extremely dull, it's exactly what you always wanted and it's exasperating, it's energizing and it's exhausting. The first year is the hardest – you're learning how to do it all, how to meet the demands of your toddler who is changing and developing all the time, and how to combine this with looking after your new baby who is also changing and developing. There can be times when you think you're simply going mad – and this is the same whether you stay at home, go back to work full time or work part time; whether you have a partner who is supportive or whether you're bringing up your children on your own. Here's what a few people said about staying sane with two:

> **Mums and dads on staying sane with two**
>
> *'I think what stopped me going over the edge was returning to work when Grace was about five months old. I went back part time and we hired a super-efficient Aussie who also used to cook for us each night.'*
>
> Clare, mother of Isabelle, Grace and Sam

'Not sure. It's hard going and I did/do lose the plot every now and then. I think it's important not to cram in too much in a day so you're not constantly rushing around.'

Chloe, mother of Oliver and Elise

'Going back to work helped, as did having a fantastic and flexible child-minder who has been with us for three-and-a-half years.'

Alex, father of Sarah, Leo and Annabel

'I'm not sure I did stay sane. I had no child care or family near by so it was pretty relentless at times. It was a hard year but you come out the other side and I now have a beautifully balanced and happy household! Myself included. My sanity was that hour that both of them would be asleep. I would turn TV/radio off and just sit in complete silence eating my lunch!'

Nancy, mother of Stan and Albie

'A very supportive husband who gave me space and time when possible – especially as I was bottle feeding, which made it easier to do. We worked as a team. A very good network of friends with similar aged children – so we set up a toddler group and met up a lot. We swapped children to give each other spare time.'

Sue, mother of Alice and Robbie

'I was very lucky to have a lot of family around and friends to talk to and visit.'

Shellie, mother of Blake and Brinley

> *'I didn't! My mother's help was fantastic though. Friends with children the same age are vital! Never pretend you are coping when you aren't.'*
>
> Vicci, mother of Olivia and Oscar
>
> *'We felt very lucky to be able to have our own healthy kids, when so many of our friends couldn't – it's good to keep sight of that.'*
>
> Millie, mother of Grace and Alice

And finally …

Remember how quickly your children grow up

The first year with two children may have started off very slowly, but time speeds up and suddenly your second child is no longer a baby. They are walking and becoming more independent every day. You are not getting woken up in the night (so many times) now, your older child may have started at preschool or be spending more time at nursery, the sheer physical hard work of life with a baby and a toddler is getting easier. Phew! You've survived and you can breathe a sigh of relief.

Or perhaps it's time to think about number three?

Useful resources

Family support charities

Home-Start is a leading family support organization for families with at least one child under five. Volunteers offer friendship and practical help to parents who may be struggling to cope.
Free info line: 0800 068 6368
www.home-start.org.uk

The NCT – or National Childbirth Trust – is the UK's biggest parenting charity. It offers support and advice to parents through pregnancy, birth and early parenthood. It also organizes antenatal and postnatal classes, and some very good nearly new sales nationwide.
Helplines: pregnancy and birth line: 0300 330 0772, breastfeeding line: 0300 330 0771, postnatal line: 0300 330 0773, enquiries line: 0300 330 0770
www.nct.org.uk

Parentline Plus is a charity that provides help and support to anyone caring for children including grandparents, step-parents and other relatives.
Helpline: 0808 800 2222
www.parentlineplus.org.uk

Breastfeeding

La Leche League aims to help mothers to breastfeed through mother to mother support. It also offers information and education.
Helpline: 0845 120 2918
www.laleche.org.uk

Twins

Tamba is a charity that provides support for families with twins, triplets and more.
Twinline is staffed by trained volunteers: 0800 138 0509
www.tamba.org.uk

Lone parent

Gingerbread is a national charity that works for and with single-parent families and provides support services.
Helpline: 0808 802 0925
www.gingerbread.org.uk

Crying babies

Cry-sis offers support for families with excessively crying, sleepless and demanding babies.
Helpline: 0845 122 8669
www.cry-sis.org.uk

Postnatal depression

House of Light is an independent charity offering free national support, advice and information about postnatal depression. They also help and give advice to the partners or carers of those with the illness.
Helpline: 0800 043 2031
www.pndsupport.co.uk

Mind is a leading mental health charity providing information and advice for promoting better mental health.
Info line: 0845 766 0163
www.mind.org.uk

Help

Doula UK Ltd is an organization run voluntarily by doulas. Doulas offer emotional and practical support for mothers before, during and after birth – their job is to 'mother the mothers'.
Information line: 0871 433 3103
www.doula.org.uk

Childcare International is one of many au pair agencies. This is the one we have used for the past five years so I can recommend it. A great deal of care is taken to find an au pair who will fit in with your family and your requirements. For us, having au pairs has been a huge help in coping with family life.
Phone: 0800 652 0020
www.childint.co.uk

Useful websites

www.mumsnet.com gives parenting tips and advice, product reviews, webchats and special offers

www.bbc.co.uk/parenting gives clear, helpful and positive advice on parenting

www.healthvisitors.com is for parents of infants and children aged zero to five and gives expert advice from health visitors on a range of topics. It also offers confidential online health visitor support

www.homebirth.org.uk provides information about home births so you can decide whether or not it's right for you

www.adviceguide.org.uk gives online help from the Citizens Advice Bureau about benefits for families and children

www.relateforparents.org.uk is a site which offers support, ideas, guidance and information for all categories of parents (step, adopted, biological) about children of any age

Index